The
Part-Time Entrepreneur
How to Run a Successful Side
Business While Working a Full-
Time Job

StartUp Mindset

Table of Contents

Introduction

In many ways, part-time entrepreneurship can be similar to full-time entrepreneurship. Most people assume that starting a part-time business is always easy. Books, blogs, and articles will tell you that you just need to follow an easy five step plan, purchase a program or invest in "this one thing". They don't tell you how to overcome the problems that you'll face. They never tell you that you're going to have to learn to balance life, work, and business. They don't tell you how to find the extra 8 hours a day it takes to find products, to sell online, manage your business finances, and market your idea. They don't tell you about the challenges you may face and the things you'll have to sacrifice.

As a part-time entrepreneur you'll still have deadlines, you'll still have customers, you'll still have products and services to sell, and you'll still have responsibilities. You still need to manage your money and manage your energy. The major difference is with part-time entrepreneurship, you just do it in less time. In this way, the part-time entrepreneur has more challenges to overcome than full-time entrepreneurs.

Part-time entrepreneurs have less time to achieve the same goals. Ask any entrepreneur that has left their job in order to run their business full-time and they'll tell you the one thing they needed more than the money was the time. This book is not going to be a "quick, get rich quick setup" or "five steps to full-time". This book is aimed at making you a successful part-time entrepreneur so that, if you choose, you can be a successful full-time entrepreneur. This book will show you how to manage your time, create ideas, innovate, and utilize technology like successful startups but in less time.

This book is about overcoming the challenges you will face: How do you find the time to run a part-time business? How to generate good ideas that will help you succeed. What to do when you start to make money. What do you do when you aren't making? Should you do it alone or should you find a partner? How do you handle the stress? How do you make the most of your time? How do you become the best entrepreneur you can be while still working a full-time job?

This book answers all of these questions and many more. Part-time entrepreneurship is where it starts. If you can learn to manage your business part-time, you are setting yourself up to have more freedom than even full-time entrepreneurs. You will be able to have the freedom to decide whether you want to keep your part-time business running for part-time income or if you want to leave your full-time job, run your business, and live your dreams.

Think of part-time entrepreneurship as training camp. It has many of the same elements as full-time entrepreneurship but with a lot less at stake. Before the NBA season, players develop their skills, work on their conditioning and prepare themselves for the season. If a player has a particular weakness that opposing teams can exploit, the offseason is the best time to work on that weakness.

This is the advantage of part-time entrepreneurship. If you have never had to deal with time constraints, how to scale a business, hiring (outsourcing or in-house) and everything else that comes with being an entrepreneur, your part-time business is the place to work on those skills. This book is for individuals who have an idea for a business but haven't the courage to start. Maybe you're thinking about developing an app, starting an eBay business or launching a landscaping venture. This book is to help you decide whether entrepreneurship is for you and if it is, how to use your free time to test the grounds of your business and yourself.

This book is also for individuals who are running a part-time business but want to take that business to the next level. Maybe there are time restraints, lack of funding, lack of resources, or lack of experience. This book will show you how to get all of those things and more.

Chapter 1

The Changing Landscape

"Life is a series of natural and spontaneous changes. Don't resist them; that only creates sorrow. Let reality be reality. Let things flow naturally forward in whatever way they like."

-Lao Tzu

Entrepreneurship Is Changing

The trend of entrepreneurship has been on the rise for several years. This trend is good news for full-time and part-time entrepreneurs alike. The 2016 Kauffman Index of Startup Activity, an annual series of reports from the Kauffman Foundation, measures startup activity on the national, state, and metropolitan level. The 2016 Index offers invaluable information about startup activity in the United States, and looks at who is starting new businesses, where they start them, and where startup communities are thriving.

Startup Activity in America

The Kauffman Index uses the Startup Activity Index to measure how many new businesses were begun in the United States in the past year in comparison to the overall adult population. In 2016, the Startup Activity Index rose to 0.38, an increase from its 2015 rate of 0.31. To break these numbers down, it means that 310 out of 100,000 adults began new businesses in 2015, and in 2016 this number rose to 330 out of every 100,000 American adults.

Entrepreneurship rose during both 2015 and 2016. Startup activity hit its lowest point in twenty years two years ago after falling dramatically during the recession. While the startup rate hasn't rebounded to its pre-recession levels quite yet, this two-year trend of increasing rates is promising.

There are more new entrepreneurs now than there were last year, and there are more entrepreneurs reporting that they decided to begin new businesses because they saw market opportunities to do so.

This trend reflects the resurgence of the American economy in the past few years, and greater opportunities for entrepreneurs to take the plunge. Small businesses and startups are an integral part of the American economy. Together, they account for half of all private sector employment, and almost two thirds of all new private sector jobs created each year. The U.S. Bureau of Labor Statistics reported that new businesses created 3 million jobs in 2016, and this number is expected to grow in 2017.

The Different Incarnations of Entrepreneurship

Do you want to be an entrepreneur, or do you just want what entrepreneurs have? This is a very valid question that all part-time entrepreneurs should ask themselves. Since entrepreneurship has some benefits that most corporate jobs do not, many in the workforce desire to start their own businesses just to get a few of the perks that entrepreneurs enjoy. But these days, it is possible to enjoy some of the benefits of being an entrepreneur without taking the plunge. Corporations are now utilizing the services of intrapreneurs and extrapreneurs to complement their corporate structure.

With more and more individuals choosing entrepreneurship, what it means to be an entrepreneur is changing as well. Traditional entrepreneurship has become much less of an exception in today's job market and much more of a career choice – the "old" ideas of a job for life and climbing the career ladder no longer exist as the only available option.

There's no doubt that being an entrepreneur can be riskier and more challenging than working for someone else, but that's exactly what makes it more exciting, interesting, and gives more control to the entrepreneur. Recently, the world has seen the rise of new breeds of entrepreneurship that combine traditional employment with entrepreneurship.

Intrapreneurship: Entrepreneurship Without the Personal Risks

The first one is a hybrid of entrepreneur and a more traditional employment arrangement. Being an "intrapreneur" combines the best of both situations – as an "entrepreneur on the inside," you're still employed by a business and take home a salary (and in all likelihood, some bonuses in addition to this) in the same way as you would have as any other type of employee. So there's more security and stability than straight-up entrepreneurship.

An example of Intrapreneurship is the now famous "Skunk Works" project. Skunk Works is another name for Advanced Development Programs or ADP. Lockheed Martin allowed Kelly Johnson, Skunk Works founder, to work as an autonomous organization with a small, focused team. That decision allowed Skunk Works to create some of the most innovative aircraft models, including the SR71. Lockhead Martin learned that successful intrapreneurship happens when team members are allowed to define a clear path with their idea and they are given the power to modify and innovate as needed, without a crazy approval process.

Intrapreneurs take risks in the same way as an entrepreneur would; only using someone else's budget and financial backing rather than their own. In the same vein, an intrapreneur may have been more commercially successful if they worked for themselves but of course, they would also be taking more personal risks and increasing their liability. This isn't always the case, however, studies have shown that as intrapreneurs aren't gambling from their own pocket, there can be an added level of detachment which could therefore actually encourage riskier strategies and a more confident decision-making process.

An intrapreneur's natural habitat is within the confines of an organization – sometimes dealing with internal politics and conflicts within an organization that an entrepreneur wouldn't have to deal with. They are usually highly skilled and specialized, whereas an entrepreneur may have more general ideas and understanding of the specific business they're based in (and employ others to fill in the gaps).

Another consideration is ownership – an entrepreneur will likely have a clear ownership of their concept and business, indeed they may feel that their business is part of them. An intrapreneur is unlikely to feel as strongly, and their ideas exist and are likely owned by, the company that they are based at as an intrapreneur. This can lead to less recognition or less equity in a venture, but this wholly depends on the business an intrapreneur is based at and how they want to recognize the contribution to their business.

Many innovative companies are working to encourage intrapreneurship and different ways of thinking among their employees to foster the passion and drive seen in an intrapreneur throughout a business. They have all the drive of an entrepreneur, but the relative safety of an employee and the benefits of economies of scale and gaining resources.

Whereas an entrepreneur might start the fire, an intrapreneur keeps it going. The stakes aren't as high, but it can provide a balance that doesn't always come with entrepreneurship – they're not afraid of risks, and are more likely than the average employee to take them. But their risks are lower than an entrepreneur's, as is the independence in decision-making. Rather than being intuitive in nature, an intrapreneur is usually restorative – helping a business to regenerate and grow.

Intrapreneurs have been key in the development of Sony, Google, Shutterstock, Java, Kodak, Toyota, Walmart, Facebook, Dreamworks, Intel and one of the most well-known office products across the globe – Post-it Notes. Spencer Silver, an employee of 3M, took advantage of the companies "bootlegging" policy which allowed employees to spend 15% of their time at work developing ideas.

Using this time, Spencer designed a light adhesive but was unsure how to use it. Five years later, one of Silver's colleagues, Art Frey, noticed bookmarks falling out of his hymnals during choir practice and remembered the product. Nothing happened with this until a marketing manager named Bill Shoonenberg spent 15% of his time driving sales. And therefore, a combined intrapreneurship approach helped to get this product onto the market.

Extrapreneur: The Entrepreneurial Hybrid

Another type of entrepreneurship that is currently on the rise is the "extrapreneur," a combination of the intrapreneur and entrepreneur. They aren't employed by a company, nor do they work completely for themselves. They act almost as a contractor who is outsourced to. Both sides guarantee a minimum level of trade and ways of working, but there isn't that tie as with being an intrapreneur or an employee. In our freelance and "side hustle" flexible economy where millennials no longer want to be tied to one company or work within the constraints of the typical employer/employee relationship, this fits in perfectly.

Again, it all comes down to a safety net. The business needs may change, the company may merge or get smaller, but the likelihood is that this "extrapreneurship" partnership will be a long-term relationship. The company benefits as they don't have to employ someone, but they still guarantee a level of expertise, delivery, and ownership.

While, in all likelihood, they don't pay what they would to bring in a contractor from the free market as they have an in-house agreement – the extrapreneur still receives the added security and both sides have the advantage of being able to approach projects more flexibly.

Extrapreneurs work to facilitate collaboration and act as change agents – across companies, organizations, sectors, and event markets. They take their innovative ideas and solutions and share them with others to benefit more widely. By approaching their role in business in this way, they're able to work on the bigger picture and help to solve large-scale problems.

Extrapreneurs can also be excellent in supporting social change, working for non-profits, and coming up with solutions to problems, collaboratively, that are too big for one person or organization to solve.

The working world, and running a successful business, is constantly fluid and changes all the time. Being able to develop skills that match the needs of a business needs, and a flexible workforce that are able to move with the business could be a winning formula to drive entrepreneurship – in all forms – in the future.

More than ever before, businesses are operating in a global market_that needs new ways of thinking and implementation to work through the challenges and opportunities that arise as a result. Entrepreneurship and innovation offer an ideal solution to meet the changing needs of business owners, customers, and the way that services are used.

Part-time Entrepreneurship

This is different than the previous 2 entrepreneurial incarnations. As a part-time entrepreneur, your primary responsibility is to your full-time job. But you have more accountability and control over your part-time business.

You get to drive and direct the business without sacrificing the security of a bi-weekly paycheck. This is both good and bad. **Good, because everyone loves the feeling of security. Bad, because security usually doesn't lead to success.**

I say usually, because it is up to the entrepreneur to determine if they truly want to succeed or stay safe. Being a part-time entrepreneur allows for a person to develop entrepreneurial skills, and test their business idea, as well as pave a path towards true freedom.

Oftentimes, we believe that when we quit our full-time paying job and venture into entrepreneurship, we will not be able to succeed. However, the solution to this is easy- instead of quitting your job, you can still work from 9-5 and build your business empire at the side until you are able to replace at least 60% of your day job income.

This may take more time than you think. Therefore, you need to be patient with the process. Building your own business should not take away from your work ethic. The only way to scale your business is putting more time into it, Ensure that you are capable of serving two masters at a time.

Due to the Great Recession in 2008, more and more people learned to start their own businesses in order to make it. Now, side businesses are being run by millions of people as a way to ease into full-time entrepreneurship or even just a way to earn awesome side income.

The Courage to Start

The Internet and bookstores have no shortage of information on the topic of entrepreneurship and business. There is a reason for this. It is because everyone has an opinion and business is not an exact science. That is the downside as well as the upside.

Because business is not an exact science, what it takes to succeed in business is hard to nail down. It is also something that constantly changes. If you are afraid of change and have no intention of fighting your fear, entrepreneurship may not be for you.

But that change is also a wonderful thing. To start a business 30 years ago was much harder than it is now. Starting a business would require a bank loan, retail space, employees, and money for advertising. Now, starting a business can be done by filling out the legal documents online, setting up a good looking small business website design, and building social media profiles to let people know about your business. That is how to start, but succeeding in business is much more than the start.

But nothing happens without the start. Ideas that sit in your brain are wasted ideas. Most people have no problem coming up with a good business idea or even a great business strategy. But neither of those things creates a successful business. Starting, building, and working your business idea is what makes the most difference. This book was designed to help you run your business as a part-time entrepreneur with as much ease and effectiveness as possible. Let's get started.

Chapter 2

The Realities of
Entrepreneurship

"A dream doesn't become reality through magic; it takes sweat, determination and hard work."

-Colin Powell

The idea of running a part-time business is attractive to many people for many reasons. The assumption is that a part-time business is easier than running a business full-time. Make no mistake about it, success, in any endeavour, is difficult.

Since the idea of a part-time business is appealing, the wave of people who want to jump in is many.

The Difference Between Side Hustling and Part-time Entrepreneurship

Side hus·tle *"Activity that brings in extra cash; something other than your main job."*

It seems as though the "side hustle" is the thing to do these days. Most likely spurred on by the "gig economy," side hustling has become a way to earn extra money while working a full-time job. Companies such as Fiverr, Uber, and Airbnb have made it possible for anyone to make some extra cash.

This book as not about side hustling. We believe in side hustling, but there is a difference between earning some extra cash and building a business while working a full-time job. There are certain responsibilities, actions, and mindsets that running a part-time business require that are not necessary in side hustling. A part-time business can be a side hustle, but you should never treat it as a side hustle.

Difference #1-Purpose

The first obvious difference between side hustling is in their purpose. The purpose of side hustling is to better your lifestyle by giving you a weekly, bi-weekly, or monthly cash infusion. With that cash, you can take a weekend trip, pay off some debts, or just save for big purchase. All good things.

You can easily make an extra $200 a month doing just about anything. It isn't as hard as you think. But if your purpose is to make $200 a month, you might as well just get a part-time job at a call center getting people to sign up for Direct TV.

The purposes of starting a part-time business are too numerous to name. But we're going to give it a shot. Here are JUST A FEW purposes for starting a part-time business:

-Turning a skill into a marketable commodity.

-Expressing a passion while generating revenue from that passion.

-Building an infrastructure which will give you the option to leave your current job.

-To build an infrastructure which will give you the option of working half of the time of your current job so that you can travel, and spend time with friends, family, and passions.

-To be able to work in your underwear.

As you can see, there are many more reasons to start a part-time business. The reasons for doing so have a much deeper and broader meaning. They tend to be more tied to who you are and what you care about, and less focused on just the money.

,

Difference #2-Design

The part-timepreneur designs their business while the side hustler is confined to their chosen side hustles' design. This is not more evident than with individuals who use Uber as a side hustle.

In January 2016, Uber drivers were up in arms when the company announced that it was slashing its fares from approximately $1.80 to $.65 in some cities. Drivers were outraged. Protesters took to the streets in cities such as New York, San Francisco, and Tampa. Many complained of not being able to make a living driving for Uber because of the changes.

This is the main reason why gigs such as Uber, Lyft, and even many multi-level marketing ventures should be side hustles, not side businesses. If you drive for Uber or Lyfe as a side hustle, and you decide to make that your business, **you are at the mercy of those who actually own those businesses**. They have the right to change policies at any time, and you will have to either adjust, or find another way to make money. If you bought this book looking for tips on how to be a better Uber driver, I'm sorry to disappoint you.

Becoming a part-timepreneur means that you design your part-time business based on what YOU want it to be. You have options. You set strategies. You make changes, if needed. And you own the business, the business does not own you.

Realities to Face If You Want to Become a Full-time Entrepreneur

Making the decision to become a full-time entrepreneur should be well-thought out and planned. Sure, the idea of being your own boss can bring satisfaction and increase your drive to transition from being an employee to an employer. However, entrepreneurship isn't always glitter and unicorns. There are so many "behind the scenes" factors that most people don't know about or consider, simply because they focus on all of the glory that comes with being able to say "I own a business,"] even if it is just a part-time business.

It's very easy to assume that the entry-level of entrepreneurship is the toughest, and that once you get past those few rough years, everything is smooth sailing. Truth be told, that entry-level of entrepreneurship isn't clearly defined with a beginning or ending period. For some, those rough periods can last a few months, while for others, those rough periods can happen for the duration of their business.

There's no "magic formula" that can predict the likelihood that your entrepreneurial journey will be smooth or complicated. The best way to determine this is to pursue your vision and be as prepared as possible for all of the challenges that may happen. Additionally, you should understand real entrepreneurship: the truths and many untold realities of being an entrepreneur, as you embark on your quest to become your own boss.

Ask any entrepreneur how many hours they work per week and you'll hear anything from four to over 100 hours. It all depends on the workload, how many "hats" they wear in their business, their personal drive, and their time management skills. When you're an employee, you work a defined eight hour shift and you get paid for those hours. You have occasional overtime hours that you can opt-in for or are assigned, as needed, by your employer. Such is not the case with entrepreneurship.

You'll work until you've completed the job or until you're satisfied. You'll work when you become inspired. You'll work when you've made mistakes that need to be corrected. You may even work on every day that ends in –day, because if you don't work, your business will feel the hit.

Most of the hours that some entrepreneurs work are unpaid hours.

Employers are obligated to pay their staff for every hour which they work. This means, when you show up to your full-time job, you get paid. Now, the entrepreneur who works from home, the coffee shop, on their mobile phone, while at the gym and anywhere else, their job is to do everything possible to get paid.

This means that those long conference calls, countless emails, PowerPoint presentations, social media posts, and anything else that you're involved in may or may not lead to a payday.

It could also mean that the work you'll do *now*, won't pay off until *later*. So if you work 80 hours this week, you may not see a dime of what you've worked for until next month or after that. It's the ebb and flow of becoming a paid entrepreneur.

Wearing Multiple Hats

Egos have no place in entrepreneurship, because at any given time you'll have to wear multiple hats. When you're the gatekeeper, that means you'll encounter everything from unruly customers and vendors, telemarketers, and bill collectors. You'll have to screen phone calls, field communications, manage your own schedule, and handle your own customer service. People will come to you for anything and everything and expect you to deliver. As the decision-maker, your sole responsibility is to make smart, well-planned, executive decisions that affect the growth or stability of your company.

Imagine having to deal with a constantly ringing phone, a hectic schedule, and then having to decide which vendors to use for your next product or service. That's a lot! Regardless, you have to manage your roles accordingly, and perform each role responsibly until you're able to hire others to take over those demanding positions.

Of course, the more you plan, learn, practice, and execute, the more you increase your chances of building something financially rewarding.

You'll notice when you build your business plan that the breakeven point is rarely in the beginning of your business due to unforeseen events and the constant improvements you'll have to make. So, don't expect your money to work for you immediately. **Entrepreneurship is an investment of time, money, and resources that matures years after you've gotten started.**

You may want to quit—several times.

Many entrepreneurs hit their proverbial brick walls several times throughout their career. The idea of quitting, laughably, becomes relaxing as your journey with entrepreneurship gets deeper.

Being an employee is like ten times easier than working for yourself. Currently, you have predictable paydays, vacation time, sick leave, conversations over the water cooler, the occasional telecommuting days, annual raises, and office parties.

If you decide to become a full-time entrepreneur, It'll be soothing to think about not having to think about everything that comes along with running a business. You may even start putting your résumé out there and even getting some leads.

However, if you're in this entrepreneurship thing for the long haul, **you'll have to snap back to reality and get back to building your business**. Sometimes, you'll need to take a break from the hustle and bustle of your business and get back to the root of your passion, which is why you started your own business in the first place. Whatever you do, don't actually quit, unless you absolutely want to or have to. Quitting never gets good results, and you won't feel better about it as time passes.

Hopefully these facts haven't scared you, but instead, they've opened your mind about what it really means to be a full-time entrepreneur. No matter what, pursue your vision and be prepared for bumps and bruises along the way. You're an aspiring entrepreneur. You were built for this.

Focusing On and Clarifying the Vision

An entrepreneur's vision keeps the business focused. The vision (a combination of ideas, strategies, and goals) lays the foundation for your decision-making, your calculated risks, and your chances of reaching profitability. When your vision becomes clouded, you become irrational, make premature decisions, and ultimately put the longevity and success of your business at risk.

It can be hard not to be swayed and tempted by trends, new ventures, and unbelievable opportunities, especially if you're experiencing lackluster sales and unfruitful marketing. However, if you can clarify your vision and do the things you need to do to keep your business on track, you'll eventually be able to make room for new ideas and pursue them individually.

If you've struggled with committing to one business idea or if you're tempted to venture into something new before the dust settles on your current ideas, here are some things to consider in clarifying your entrepreneurial vision:

Answer the tough questions

What is it that you really want to do? How will you do it? How will it benefit your consumers? How will it benefit you? These are the core questions that make up your vision. Spend time honing in on the answers and not settling with quick responses that sound good, but don't have value. You'll come to realize that it takes time, patience, thoughtfulness, and great planning to really answer these questions. It takes even more to execute them with precision and purpose. Speaking of execution—

Execute your vision intentionally

Execution is of utmost importance, because making a plan on your computer will not suffice. It happens with most of us that we make plans with great enthusiasm, and then it doesn't take us long to drift away from it. We ignore and tread a course not known by us. We always have to remember that during the journey, we may enter unknown territories, and we not only need sound and stable plans but also contingency plans for unwarranted situations.

Some entrepreneurs get distracted by bigger ideas and easier routes, so they don't execute their existing ideas with intention. **Essentially, they don't take all of the necessary actions to see their ideas come to life the way that they're intended to.** When a vision has been muted due to distractions, lack of interest, and lack of passion, the vision suffers and so does the business. Be very clear and intentional about how you want your business to perform and what you want to happen. That way, you can make note of anything that's standing in the way of what you want and take the proper steps to fix it.

Don't Over Analyze

Have you ever over-analyzed something in your business so much that you a) can't make a decision, b) make the wrong decision, or c) want to bail on the business because it's just easier to cut the strings than to fix things. If this is you, then chances are you're suffering from analysis paralysis. When you can't figure out a situation, instead of analyzing it to death or jumping ship, turn to trusted advisors, revisit your business plan (because you *do* have one, right?), or step away for a few moments. Getting back to the root of your vision should alleviate so many of those pesky complications.

Trust yourself and Stick to It

Doubt plays a significant role in whether entrepreneurs finish what they start. If you doubt your vision and doubt the process, you ultimately doubt your likelihood of success. Every business experiences setbacks and challenges. The ones that defeat them do so because of a clear vision and a can-do attitude. Keep moving through your business—even if things slow down or become a tad more complicated. Stay committed to your idea and make modifications based on what the market demands—not because you don't believe in yourself or your idea.

Repeat after me: Vision. Action. Commitment. You need to clarify your vision for your business, act on it, and commit to it— regardless of what's going on around you and regardless of how business is looking now. You'll have slow sales months. You'll have unruly customers. You'll have everything that every other business experiences on their route to success (and most still experience it although they have highly successful business models). It's just the way business is. However, if you don't complete every part of this process (vision, action, commitment) you won't get far with much of anything.

Change is good—but only when change is going to improve a situation or introduce a better solution. If you're changing your vision simply because you're bored with it or impatient, you're creating an awful habit that won't lead to a finished result or successful reward. Adjust your business when it's necessary (because you haven't made money or you're losing money despite all of your strategic efforts). Other than that, just keep going and enjoying the rollercoaster of a ride called *entrepreneurship*.

Balance your ideas and expectations

You got into business because you had a great idea that you think will make a lot of money and create a big splash. Not every business comes off the ropes swinging. If you become disappointed that you weren't immediately the "next big thing," then you'll struggle with clarifying your vision and strategically moving towards bigger goals. Balance your current situation with your long-term goals. Just because you aren't where you want to be today doesn't mean you won't be there soon.

Chapter 3

Passion and Profits

"Passion is needed for any great work, and for the revolution, passion and audacity are required in big doses."

-Che Guevara

Passion has been understood as a romantic term for most of us. There is a passion to drive all of us in this world. This passion has been misunderstood too; however, this passion is nothing but a powerful and deep feeling of enthusiasm for something that brings satisfaction and joy to us.

So many part-time entrepreneurs are looking to take a skill or talent and turn it into cash in their bank accounts. So they start a business that is based on a particular passion. Although being passionate about a business will most certainly help that business succeed, passion is not enough; it is never enough.

Normally, we are passionate about food, music, art, sports, and a lot of other things. Entrepreneurs are usually passionate about their work because we know that if we combine work with passion, it has the capability to create miracles. When we have enthusiasm, we work harder, more efficiently, and always strive to reach higher goals, and improve ourselves to gain perfection. We compete with our own self and excel at the high standards set by us. This makes our competition healthy, and we get our rewards by getting paid for our hard work.

Anyone who says that passion is enough to make money flow

into your life, however, was probably just trying to sound positive, and probably did not try it out himself.

Many people have followed their heart to do best what they love the most. It is easy to pursue it at a great pace in the beginning; however, it soon wears out if other elements of accomplishing success are absent.

People wait endlessly to gain what they want until the end because there is hope that someday someone who recognizes talent will reward them for all the hard work and passion that they carry in their heart for what they have been pursuing. It goes wrong at times!

People Don't Care About Your Passion...Yet

Generally, not many people care about your passion and what you do with it. Their main point of interest is to find what they get out of what you do. It may be shocking for some, and set a process of serious thinking for others.

That's what successful entrepreneurs understand and those who struggle don't. The marketplace does not care that you want to work your own hours, lay on the beach, and rub lotion on your belly, or even that you love your business to death. What your potential customers care about is their problems and how you're going to solve them.

What you need the most for following your heart towards the passion you have is to be extremely good at it. If you are amazingly good, exceptionally smart at your passion, you have a fair chance of succeeding, however, if you are not, it isn't the game for you.

Before you hit "send" on the angry email you're thinking about writing, I'm not saying passion is not important. It's passion PLUS other things that create a successful venture. Here some things to couple with the love of your business to give yourself a better shot at breaking through.

Analyze

When you become an entrepreneur, you essentially become your own product, and just like any other product that you manufacture, you have to be able to judge what that product can do. You may have a passion, but can that passion produce AND can you take it from passion to profit.

You have to differentiate between desires and passion. You have to analyze what you've got to offer to the world. Mere browsing through the Internet may be good for you but not for the world, and do not expect people to be interested in what you love to do. You have to have something that is capable of bringing something to others' lives.

Mark the Milestones

Plan for the vision that you are carrying in your mind. Then mark the milestones that you are going to touch during your journey. Simultaneously, mark the success parameters and scales that are going to show during your initial journey the rate of success that you are accomplishing.

Maximum Effort

Hard work is often never talked about when passion is mentioned. Since hard work is not a feeling and is defined differently for everyone, we suggest you put in maximum effort. Once you've reached the effort of your mind, talent, and work input, look at ways you can get the most out of those things. You don't ever want to fail with the feeling that there was more you could have done to succeed.

sustainable, and will eventually drive us out of business if we let it.

At the same time, it is important to stay passionate about what you love. Turning your attention fully to making a profit can be a disaster. Thinking only about the money made can drive you to compromise quality and loyalty to your customers. It may also cause you to lose the love that you had when you started.

The key is to find a balance between passion and profit. If you are completely engrossed in your passion, then it may be a good idea to get a partner who can handle the accounting. That way, you can focus on creating the product while your accountant handles the finance.

Business Urban Legends

If you network with new entrepreneurs, you will eventually run into some business myths. I call them business urban legends. I have to admit that when I first began to monetize my passion, I believed some of these myths were true. I even repeated them because I heard someone else say them.

Now that I have more experience, I realize that many of the people who spread these myths may have just been making excuses for their unsuccessful ventures. Myths about business spread faster than the flu. It is important to know what to believe and what not to believe. Here are a few of the more common business myths that you will come across.

If you do what you love, the money will come- I think I've heard this one more than any other myth. It's a nice thought, but it's just not true. There are many very talented writers and singers who struggle to make a living while they are doing what they love. It is great to do what you want to make a living from it, but at some point you will have to create a way to make it profitable.

My talent/product/service is so good that it will sell itself-No matter what your talent is, you will need to market it in order for it to be successful. You could be a great singer, but you will never land that multimillion dollar record deal if you only sing in the shower and in your car. You would need to do something so that people can hear you sing. You may need to perform at an open mike or get your demo into the hands of as many people as possible.

If you build it, they will come-Wouldn't it be nice to be able to open a store, build a website, or design a product, and then just sit back and watch the money roll in. In the real world, it takes much more than that. Building a Facebook page, Shopify store, or anything else does not guarantee that anyone will care. It is up to you to make the people care.

Failure is bad-Failure is an obstacle much like any other obstacle you will face. Instead of thinking of failure as the end of the road, consider it an opportunity to find another route to your destination.

All I need is a good idea-Ideas are good but not enough. It takes work, strategy, and funding to get any good idea off the ground. That is why most venture capitalists will not fund an idea. They usually require a track record, detailed business plan, and exceptional growth potential before they invest.

Someone else has already done it so I can't do it-One example where this is not true is with the Apple iPod. MP3 technology was patented in 1989. Many years before the iPod came around, but not too many people took notice. Apple took an existing technology, gave it a clever name, made it easy to use by creating iTunes, and made it cool to own. Presto, billions of dollars in sales. It's not about being first, but finding a way to appeal to the market and creating a better product.

Turning Passion into Profits

1. Do Your Research

It is important to know if people will pay for what you have to offer. Doing market research will let you know if there is a demand. You may have a talent for making picnic baskets out of old shoe laces, but is anyone willing to pay for that? It is equally important to target and analyze your clientele so that you are not wasting money on advertising. Market research will also tell you who you should be marketing to.

2. Find your Unique Selling Point (USP)

Your USP is what differentiates you from your competition. There must be a reason why people would be willing to pay for what you have to offer instead of going somewhere else for it. We all have something unique about us. Try to find what makes you unique, and use that to your advantage.

3. Evaluate Your Passion Objectively

Or better yet, have someone else do it for you. Even though you have a good idea for a business or you have a talent, you must know if it can be profitable enough to make a living. Look at your skill or passion, and be honest with yourself to evaluate whether there is a money-making opportunity.

When you evaluate yourself, you will better understand what you may be able to accomplish. The host of the Food Network's "Good Eats" Alton Brown once said that before someone can take a risk to go out on their own, they must evaluate themselves. "It is important that you evaluate yourself" Brown says, "because you are about to become a product and it's important to know what that product can do."

4. Develop Your Talent

Talent is a marvelous thing to have, but it is not enough. In the book "Talent is Overrated: What really Separates World-Class Achievers From Everybody Else," Geoff Colvin writes about what extraordinary achievers do in order to be successful. He notes that, -although talented, overachievers seem to practice and develop their talents more than the average person. He concludes that the development of talent is the real reason some succeed while other don't.

This idea is echoed in the book Talent is Never Enough by John C Maxwell. He puts a high value on talent, but points out that talent and skill are two different things. If you have a talent that you would like to make profitable, begin developing it immediately!

5. Learn the Industry

Learn as much as you can about the industry that you are going into. If you are opening a retail shop, then you should learn all that you can about retail. You should begin to build relationships with manufacturers as well as distributors.

You may also want to begin to associate with other people in your line of business. Surround yourself with people who are where you want to be. Begin to think about the business the same way they do. Once you understand the business space that you are in, find a way to be better than everyone else that is doing it.

6. Understand Your Cost

You may be making $10,000 per month, but if it's costing you $9,500 to operate, you're not doing very well. Figure all of your costs-including your salary-for the business so that you can gauge how profitable it really is. Understanding your cost also means understanding how valuable your time, energy, and talent are.

Note: Your U.S.P will also help you determine how much you are really worth.

7. Spread the Word

Get the word out about your passion. If you think your talent or skill is worth something, the world should know about it. Build a website, start a blog, and begin marketing yourself. If you are a performer, get in front of as many people as possible. No one will know about your talents unless you tell them.

8. Stick With it

Sometimes, success is right around the corner. Just because you didn't make money in the first three months doesn't mean you should quit. Most businesses take a little time before they are profitable.

Chapter 4

Being a Solopreneur and Co-founding

"Life is like the monkey bars: you have to let go to move forward. Once you make the decision to leap into entrepreneurship, be sure to loosen your grasp on old concepts so you can swing your way to new ones."

-Leah Busque

Most part-time entrepreneurs start out as solopreneurs. Solopreneurs are entrepreneurs who run their business alone. The goal of just about every business is to grow. Growth usually includes partners, full time employees, and other lines of business. However, there are many, many other benefits of growing your company on your own.

As a solopreneur, you will have full control over different aspects of the business.There is no need to consult other directors or anyone else before making a decision in your business when you are the boss. This will also limit your chances of compromising with your decisions simply because some of your directors are not comfortable.

Running your business alone may also benefit your customers. Smaller companies usually have a better reputation of addressing customer issues than their larger counterparts. Being a soloentrepreneur allows you to be closer to your customer, which in turn creates great customer loyalty.

Being closer to your customer makes it easy to respond to the needs of customers in the best manner possible. Timely responses to complaints made by your customers increases the chances of retaining them as well as attracting new customers. On the other hand, companies take time to address concerns made by their customers.

Many solopreneurs are freelancers which makes their services highly sought after. In a 2014 Oxford Economics survey commissioned by SAP, 83% of executives planned on using freelancers over the next three years. That's most likely you. With more specialized services and businesses being developed, specialized services are also required.

Depending on your business outlook, it is possible that your business will remain a one person show. We understand that there is an endless list of reasons why teams and partnerships could help your business. But it is equally important to know your business so well that you know whether or not finding a co-founder is right for you.

Let's say that in the future, you may decide to leave your full-time job to run your business full-time. But because of unforeseen circumstances, the business does not work out. As a solopreneur, you can easily slip back into the workforce and restart your career or just to buy yourself some more time to grow the business. If you have co-founders and shareholders to be accountable to, slipping in and out of a job is not possible.

The solopreneur has the opportunity to test the waters before making any decision. This makes them able to avoid any unnecessary risks that they are likely to encounter in the process of venturing into the new business.

Let's look at the benefits of running your business yourself, as well as how to find the right co-founder for your startup.

Benefits of Flying Solo

Quick to Start and Low Startup Cost

Starting a business with your friends or any other person can be very difficult. You have to sit down and discuss various issues before making any move. This is not the case when you run the business as an individual. There is no need to move up and down all in the name of registering your business with the necessary legal authorities.

However, you will be required to inform the local government about your intentions as well as obtain a license that will allow you to legally continue with your daily operations. Large businesses usually require the services of a lawyer to get going. Solopreneurs can get away with using a service such as Incfile.com or Legalzoom.com that will charge $50 to take care of your legal paperwork for you. You could literally have a business idea and be in business in a few days. Can't get any quicker than that.

If you wanted to sell (or resell) products to the general public 20 years ago, you used to have to open a physical store. That would mean a cost for buying the products, store rental cost, shelves cost, cash registers, the list goes on. These days, you can sign up with Shopify for about $30 and set up an online store to sell whatever you want.

Capital required to start a sole business is less compared to a large company. Which is why part-time entrepreneurs generally go it alone at first. Some of the common costs that a multi-person business incurs include equipment, training, insurance, facility rental, etc. The average overall cost of a new business according to sba.gov is $30,000. Do you have that lying around?

Conversely, a soloentreprneur, part-time, or freelancing business can begin for as little as $100. Some businesses can start with almost nothing. **Beware however, there is a correlation between a low barrier of entry and high failure rates for some businesses.** Since the cost of starting of business is so low, some solopreneurs don't take it as serious as someone who invested their life savings. You still have to run your business like you've invested $100,000 if you want to be successful.

Privacy

Privacy is an issue of great concern when running any type of business. Keeping information secret in a limited company is not an easy task. Shareholders, creditors, and other parties would want to know more about your profit, capital, expenses, and other business activities. If privacy is a big issue on your side, then you need to start and run a business yourself.

A solopreneur can keep information about how much money he or she makes from the business for years without the knowledge of others (besides the IRS). In addition, she or he can handle any issues facing the business in secrecy, thus maintaining the confidence of both the loyal and potential customers.

Easy Accounting

The processing of accounting for funds within the business is easier when you are running the operations solely. There is no need to have formal corporation tax returns or Annual Accounts. You can keep your financial records in any manner as long as it suits your needs.

In addition, it is not mandatory to submit details of the amount of profit you have been making for the past months to anyone for auditing purposes. You basically handle all your accounts without external interference from another party. I recommend the book "Small Time Operator: How to Start Your Own Business, Keep Your Books, Pay Your Taxes, and Stay Out of Trouble." It is perfect for someone who doesn't know anything about accounting but is running a small business,

No Salary Cap

Companies make a lot of profit when compared to sole proprietors. However, the huge sums of profit generated by companies are divided among the different shareholders of the company. This leaves each member with a very little amount to take home.

A Solopreneur retains the entire profit his or her business will make within a particular financial period. A good number of entrepreneurs who own a business on their own do not like the idea of employing huge numbers of people with their investment. This makes them incur fewer costs while at the same time maximizing the amount of profits they generate.

In addition to profit retention, these individuals can also retain their personal assets that were being used in the daily operations of the business. The profit retained by the business can be used to open other business ventures or any other purpose depending on the Solopreneur.

Major Challenges of Solopreneurship

Spreading Yourself Too Thin

One of the major challenges of running your business on your own is the chance of burnout. Having a full-time job is hard enough, but being a part-timepreneur on top of that can be a bit much if you do not know how to handle it. If you decide to run your business alone, you will have to master the art of prioritizing your work. This is the only way to make sure that the important things get done, while not spreading yourself too thin.

When the biggest most important tasks get done, the little stuff usually doesn't derail us. This issue arises when large amounts of time is spent on stat checking, answering email, and non-focused social media marketing. When all the energy is spent on these things that do not have a large impact, less energy is spent on the tasks that will have that impact.

Because you have your work responsibilities and your part-time businesses' you need to make sure that your time is well spent. Part-time businesses with co-founders usually have a balance between the founders that offset important tasks and milestones so that one person does not go crazy trying to do it all. Before deciding to run your business alone, you need to have a plan to avoid spreading yourself too thin.

Weaknesses Must Become Strengths

The other major challenge you will face when running your business alone is the challenge of mastering all of the hats you will wear. As a solo, part-time entrepreneur, you will be the sales department, creative team, social media manager, administrative assistant, operations manager, and every other position your part-time business may need that day.

The good news about part-time businesses is that they do not need all of these positions all of the time. But at some point in your journey, you will have to put on another hat. You must get used to making your weaknesses your strengths. It does not make sense to be a creative genius or an operational savant, if you can't sell what your business has to offer.

In businesses that are comprised of a team, even those that are being operated part-time, it makes sense that a person's responsibilities should coincide with their strengths. In a part-time business, you must develop strengths in all areas.

Teaming up -Finding a Co-founder

Having a good co-founder with the same vision may help drive your business. Guy Kawasaki suggests that a co-founder should also have the same commitment to that vision as you.

However, your co-founder should be different than you in other areas such as expertise and perspective.

Before you go looking for someone to help you run the business, you need to have a clear idea of what you are looking for in a co-founder. Just because someone is interested in your idea doesn't necessarily mean that they are right for your startup. Even though there are plenty of reasons why it is better to run your company alone, there is great value in having a co-founder.

Cast a Wide Net

This may seem like basic, generic advice, but it works. Tap into your personal network of connections and people you know, and try to expand on it as much as you possibly can. For a start, let everyone in your social and business circle know you're trying to find a co-founder for your startup.

Casting a wide net will enable you to reach out to a large number of people, most of who you probably know personally, which means you will minimize the risk of hiring someone whose skills, mindset, and habits you're not too familiar with. High school friends, people you attended a university with, former colleagues, former competitors, former vendors, your friends' friends...the possibilities are limitless.

There are countless ways to go about networking, but the point is to let as many people as possible know about your business, needs, and ideas. This is the old school way of networking – word of mouth marketing will never go out of style, no matter what people say. Hang out with individuals who might be of use to your business, and attend industry events.

In short; become visible and talk to people about your business and whatever you're passionate about. Your best bet to find a co-founder is to advertise your enthusiasm and entrepreneurship organically and verbally, before demonstrating it on paper. Casting a wide net may only be the beginning, but it is certainly a solid foundation and the perfect breeding ground for your personal network of valuable connections.

Search for a Contrast to Complement Yourself

What does a good business partner or, in this case, a co-founder, need to have in order for your joint venture to function well? Simply put, he or she needs to have what you do not have. People with complementary personalities and skill sets make a good partnership. Someone who fills the gaps in your experience and skill sets, while challenging your views and offering a different perspective is the perfect co-founder and business partner. Ideally, your partner should not confirm your vision, instead they should expand and complement it, therefore make you think your every decision through by challenging your opinions.

Business relationships like these are often fiery and sometimes even a double-edged sword, but if you and the co-founder of your startup manage to strike a balance and manage to find a way to work together in synergy, masking each other's flaws and complementing each other's skills, your office will be constantly brimming with new ideas and concepts. It is not easy to find a person like this, so make sure to spend time with people you think are good candidates. Get to know them on a personal level, and get familiar with their thought process and habits.

Obviously, someone who contradicts and counterattacks your ideas is the best match, but there are things that you need to have in common for your startup to grow and expand – you and your partner need to share vision, values, and principles regarding the way your firm operates. You need to aim at the same target and have the same objective and end goal, even if your modus operandi is different.

Focus on Online Networking Sites Where Founders Roam

No matter how effective working your environment and establishing "real life" connections is, a lot of business is happening online these days. In fact, large sums of money move online in this day and age, and many companies exist and function solely online. Servers are the new office buildings, websites are marketing tools, and various social media platforms are where connections are made and businesses are started.

Platforms such as LinkedIn are a good place to start, but micro-niche online communities and other social media websites can be equally as efficient. There are several sites that now offer an opportunity to meet with Co-Founders across the world. Here are a few of the top sites:

Founders2Be

Founderdating

Cofounderslab

Instead of meeting at a bar or a restaurant, people meet, talk, and develop business ideas on forums and online communities. Being a part of this abundant world of information, connections, and business ventures is a must if you want to find a co-founder for your startup.

In order to find a co-founder online, you need to make your intentions clear and present your ideas in a concise, yet elaborate manner. Everything depends on how you present yourself and your business. There are many similarities between networking online and networking offline, but the key difference is the fact that you cannot muscle and network your way through an entire online community – developing a good social media presence, building a website around your startup, creating a bio page, participating in forum discussions, and bringing value to online communities you're a part of is challenging, but definitely a long-term investment that pays off in the long run.

Additionally, tweak and improve your social media (especially LinkedIn) profiles and try to get your name out there, make yourself known to people in your industry and try to subtly convey your skills, expertise, goals, and aspirations.

Search for Ex-Competitors; Current Coworkers

You may be able to snag yourself an awesome addition to your founding team by looking at the folks that you are competing with. Sometimes, the leaders, engineers, and salespeople from those other businesses are a good source that you can tap into to build your co-founding team. The founders of KnowEm.com ,Michael Sterko and Barry Wise, met when they were competitors trying to dominate the same SEO terms.

Ex-Competitors often understand the space you are in and will understand what needs to be done to drive your business forward. But would a competitor change sides to join a new, unproven startup? It happens more often than you may think. In 2012, the founders of Paypal, Peter Thiel and Elon Musk, backed a competing payment processing startup called Stripe.

There may be several different businesses that you have, are currently or are going to be competing with. Take a look at past members of startups that are in your space and may be your competition. Begin to research those individuals who may be a good fit for your startup, and you may find your perfect match.

The coworkers that you associate with everyday may also be a good place to look for a co-founder. One of the reasons why this is a great place to start is because of the simple fact that you are already working with that person. This means that you have an idea of their work ethic, morality, work style and expertise. Using your current pool of coworkers as a possible cofounders can be risky if the partnership does not work out, but can be extremely beneficial.

Date Before You Marry

You may be thinking that the person you found is going to be a good addition because they have passion, a like vision, and even the experience to take your startup to the next level. But this is why so many founders end up parting ways. A co-founding relationship is just that; a relationship.

And just like any relationship, it is best to take things slow and date before you commit. Your business partnership may last years, so taking the time to learn each other's strengths, weaknesses, and leadership styles is a good idea.

There are few ways that you can "date" your potential co-founders before you embark on startup matrimony. First, you may want to consider partnering on smaller business projects together. Many engineers will work for a visionary founder on a contract or freelance basis. This gives each person an opportunity to work together to see if there is synergy and if both individuals are able to take a project to success.

Another way to court your possible co-founder is to have an argument. Jessica Alter, CEO of FounderDating, suggests to The Harvard Business Review that how co-founders fight is a key metric in predicting success of a founding team. It is probably not a good idea to start an argument unnecessarily, but it is wise to not run from conflict. Learning to argue the right way will come in handy later if the stress and pressure of the business spill over and causes more serious confrontations.

Chapter 5

Using Existing Infrastructures

"Start where you are. Use what you have. Do what you can."

-Arthur Ashe

Part-time entrepreneurship's beauty is in its simplicity. There should be no need for expensive lawyers, complicated business software, or hiring marketing experts. At least there is no need for those when you first start. As your business grows, so should your support and resource needs. In this chapter, we are going to show you how to use existing tools and infrastructures to get your business up and running quickly and easily.

Running a successful startup is not easy, especially if you do not have the right skills. The first stages of developing a business are easier as well as more affordable than most entrepreneurs think. With the many tools available online, running a startup part-time should not be a daunting task. Here are some of the tools you need to begin and run a successful startup.

1. Legal Tools-Incfile & Legalzoom

With varying business structures and licensing requirements in different states, coming up with the legal structure of your startup can be very tricky. It is important to consider the idea of hiring professional and experienced staff members to provide you with legal advice. This will help avoid many legal issues that are likely to arise along the way.

Use a service such as Incfile.com to get your business up and running quickly instead of using a lawyer. Filing the necessary legal paperwork is about $49. After your business is up, you may want to use Legalzoom for contracts and other documents. Keep in mind that as you grow, you will need professional advice and guidance.

Dynamic Website for Your Business

Websites play a very important role when it comes to operating a startup. A good website should have a great landing page where your potential customers can easily find out more about your products and services. Ensure that the site is easy to navigate and offers great mobile as well as web interfaces.

Weebly(weebly.com) is probably the easiest option for a quick website set up. The have a free option which is ok but if you are running a business, you are better off paying the $12 for a more professional site and your own domain name. You can also host using WordPress, which has many themes, but for some of the customization, you may need the help of a developer.

Wix (wix.com)-A good option, but stay away from free version if you want to look professional.

Bluehost (bluehost.com)-A great option, but usually better for blogging.

Hostgator (hostgator.com)-Another good option similar to Bluehost.

1and1 (1and1.com)-A hosting option that has a free blog and website builder. Not the greatest available, but very easy to use.

Management Software-Quickbooks

Managing the operations of your business is no longer something that should make you have sleepless nights. Once you begin looking like some of the leading companies within the country, you need to behave like they do. Management software such as QuickBooks online makes financial management easy and cheap.

You only need a computer or laptop and Internet connection to get started. With time, you can upgrade to better platforms that will make securing data easy.

Storage of Digital Documents-Google Drive

Gone are the days you had to worry about losing your documents, thanks to digital storage. You can use the cloud to safely store your important files. Storing documents in the cloud makes it easy to collaborate as well as share them. Google Drive allows you to store up to 15 GB of data without paying a single dollar. Unless you want to produce or store many files, Google Drive has adequate space. This will go a long way to help save more space within your office.

Client Email Marketing-Aweber or Mailchimp

.The use of autoresponders and list builders has increased tremendously in the recent past. The leading ones are Aweber and Mailchimp. These tools are great for keeping up with your customers and creating campaigns to market to them.

The interface offered by Mailchimp is quite flexible and user-friendly. However, this user interface makes Mailchimp slower than Aweber. One of the key benefits of Aweber over Mailchimp is that is offers excellent tracking. You can see a detailed report including the exit links clicked by the users in the case of Aweber.

On the other hand, Mailchimp has no such option, and it simply highlights the users who clicked your link with a star. However, Mailchimp offers a free version which can be used for an email campaign for up to 500 subscribers. It does the job, but not as dynamically as the Aweber base version.

Phone Communication-Grasshopper

For part-time entrepreneurs or if you are a solopreneur, it is important to keep business and personal separate when it comes to communication. You also want to present a professional image to your customers, clients, and vendors. We recommend Grasshopper for that.

Grasshopper allows you to keep your number but also get a 1-800# or a local number for your business. You also set up customized extensions, make calls showing your grasshopper number, read voicemail, and forward calls so that you do not have to be in the office all the time.

I personally like Grasshopper because it makes me even more mobile. It's really cool to have, and you can try it out for free. Paid plans are still reasonably priced, starting at $12 a month.

In conclusion, before you put your startup idea into action, it is good to equip yourself with the relevant tools. Some of the tools that will make it easy to run your business include social media, phone, computer, and branding among others.

Getting Started: Social Media Checklist

Instead of breaking down each social media platform, we decided to give you a list of best practices that you can apply to any social media platform. Marketing is not an exact science. And the fact is that social media marketing is so relatively new, there are no rules that are set in stone.

The good news is that a part-time entrepreneur has a fair shot to build a successful business by using only social media as a marketing tool. We would not recommend it, but it is possible. There are, however, a few things you need to understand about that possibility. For one, it will not come while using the platforms as casually as a 60 year old grandmother of 6 who uses Facebook every now and then to post pictures of her granddaughter's 9th birthday. Your usage has to be intentional.

In this chapter, we've also included some lesser known tools that may be right for you in helping you run your part-time business with a smaller time requirement.

So often we expect change to happen quickly and in some business endeavors it does, but without unlimited marketing dollars, social media is not one of those situations. Amy Morin, a Forbes contributor who writes mainly about the psychological aspects of business describes the process of change in <u>five</u> <u>stages</u>.

1. Precontemplation
2. Contemplation
3. Preparation
4. Action
5. Maintenance

If you are reading this, you have probably passed stages one and two. According to Morin, precontemplation is when you are not yet aware that you need to change or are unwilling to accept guidance from others who are already contemplating a solution. However, if you are in stage two, contemplation, wondering if your hard work will be worth the effort, this article will get the ball rolling—or dribbling, if you will.

Preparation

Your social media company account page is your face, storefront, and introduction to your brand to potential followers, and better yet, customers. Step one should be to have an attractive bio.

Although the bio section length may change depending on the site, your bio should always easily describe your brand, tell how your brand is different, and use keywords that are accurate to what you plan to share.

Social networks are an extension to your brand, and should be designed in that same fashion. Use of branded colors and imagery are crucial to creating a consistent brand message. Header image and profile images are important too. People want to be able to get to know you better, but they can't do that by looking at the Twitter default "egg" image.

Create a base.

Make sure to post a few times before you start following and interacting with others. If you only have a few posts on your account, make sure the posts are concurrent to each other and to your brand's message. Be as precise and consistent as possible with your first posts. If you are in the business of pet grooming and sell natural products on your website, perhaps your first few posts should include topics such as treating stinky pets, grooming frequency, and the harmfulness of chemically-enriched products.

Action

It's all about who you know.

Social media is all about increasing your followers so that when you have something to share, your post can be seen. To be seen right off the bat, go ahead and dust off that old Rolodex and start inviting your contacts who you've known for years to connect. Personalization is key to email marketing, and readers respond quicker and are more willing to interact when they recognize the person or brand on the other side of the screen. LinkedIn is especially good at using your data to find connections with people you already know, but with a little effort you can grow your social media presence using this tactic on every social network.

Follow wisely.

The more targeted you are, the better. Building a quality following online is a tough task because instead of solely adding numbers to a tally, you are finding like-minded people who have similar interests, and in doing so will find connections with people most likely to purchase your product. Be interactive and don't forget to like things! Ask questions and start conversations. A short comment on a tweet or post can go a long way.

But more than anything, to be followed you have to share topics readers will find value in and follow others who you find share valuable information so that you can better educate others with it. It is the bigger the better with social media, and to gain a following quickly it is more efficient to follow and interact with accounts that will be seen by the largest number of people. Follow accounts that have strong retweets, shares, and engagement numbers, and then piggy-back on their success.

Build real relationships.

If you are interested in others, there is a good chance they will be interested in you. Tag people in photos and in posts when applicable to call out a job well done or to encourage conversation. Be honest and let your followers know what your likes, dislikes, or thoughts are, and chances are they will share their preferences with you too.

Maintenance

If at first you don't succeed, keep trying. And if at first you do succeed, still keep it up. It is important to note that at if you first see movement one way or the other, you must understand that social media success is a process.

Optimize loyal followers.

Do your followers know you have accounts on other social networking sites? Do they follow you everywhere? Make it known and make it worth it! A complete list of social media accounts should be easily accessible everywhere your readers interact with you. Proudly display your social network links on your website, email footer, business card, corporate advertising, and any other way you can think. If you have a growing presence on Twitter, why not share a tweet promoting your Pinterest account? Use the attention you have gained on one network to build your following elsewhere.

Share the love.

Respond to new followers with direct messages and share tweets that you especially like. A thank you can go a long way, and a direct message saying thanks for the new follow can spark a new conversation you may have never received.

The proof is in the pudding

Your goal is to establish enough social proof that you attract followers due to the sheer idea that if they did not follow you they would be missing out on valuable information. Accounts with an extremely large following, usually over 10,000 followers, start to build on this status because people look at the amount of your followers and are influenced by the fact that if you are followed by so many people, they should too because of an instinctual fear of missing out.

Getting there is the hard part– a process that is developed, earned, and worked on overtime.

Social Media-Lessor known resources

For those of you who want to take your social media activities to the next level, this section is for you. Basic social media is easy to do, since most people understand its basic prowess and functions. This is where some people make the mistake of judging whether or not a specific social media platform is right for their business.

The problem with that approach is that not all social media activities equate favorable results. Also, a certain strategy that creates awareness and visibility for your business may be ostracized and seen as spam on another platform. This is why it is important to approach each platform with caution and respect the platform for what it is; a community creator.

Once you understand the language of that community, you can then begin to apply different methods and actions that will breed desired outcomes for your business.

Just as every new startup grows, so should your social media efforts. As you drive toward your goals and pave new roads through your entrepreneurial zeal, remember these three aspects to approaching social media.

1: Grow at All Costs – The Scrappy Approach

Budgetary constrictions are a huge barrier to a startup, and resourcefulness is crucial. Unless you're backed by a large trust fund that just kicked into gear, you're going to need to find ways to affordably promote your brand. Whether you are strapped for cash or time, it is important to utilize some of the incredible social media management platforms available online.

Start automating with these three top social media management tools:

Hootsuite

With over 10 million users and counting, Hootsuite is one of the most recognized online platforms. Get started for free and link your business to 35 popular networks including Facebook, Twitter, YouTube, LinkedIn, and Instagram. You don't have to be a social media pro to use the platform. Don't forget to learn smart social media best practices and grow your brand online with Hootsuite Academy.

Scrappy Capabilities: Hootsuite allows brands to stay organized while growing their presence on social media. Up to the second social media analytics make tracking engagement and marketing objectives a breeze.

Cost: Free to get started with up to 3 social profiles, analytics, and scheduling. Pro and Business plans start at $9.99/month with a 30-day free trial and include bulk scheduling vanity URLs, publishing approval workflows, and custom set-up and training.

Likeable Hub

This management platform boasts its powerful ability to build, engage, and grow with social media marketing. Available social media networks include Facebook, Twitter, and LinkedIn to help generate referral business and sales leads.

Scrappy Capabilities: Ever wonder what your customers are saying about your brand online? Likeable Hub can automatically manage your reputation with listening tracking, and brands can respond by sharing stories directly to their social media accounts. **Cost**: Likeable's free version is fairly standard with basic reporting and scheduling tools, but where Likeable really stands out is its content sharing and post ideas. With over 1,000 post ideas to get your creative juices flowing, users with even the smallest amount of time can get their social media accounts up and running and quickly start gaining followers.

Buffer

Schedule your posts complete with up to four images at a time to one or many social media networks. The link shortening and optimal timing tool enables users to create social media posts that are both simple and scheduled for a time that is just right to capture the attention of your target audience.

Scrappy Capabilities: According to Inc.com, 81 percent of people only skim the content they read online and usability expert, Jakob Nielsen, claims that the average user reads just 20 to 28 percent of words during an average visit (which coincidentally is about the length of this section of the chapter at this point). How do you gain a reader's attention and keep it? WebDAM addresses the issue of our fleeting attention span in a recent study, reporting that posts with videos attract 3X more links, and ones with images produce 650 percent higher engagement than text-only posts.

Buffer's scrappy capability for visual content creation is paramount, but instead of telling you I will show you the Buffer difference.

Cost: Accounts range from "individual," which is free, to "awesome" that is $10/month, and agency pricing runs from $99-$399. Although users are limited to just 10 scheduled posts per profile with the free account, a marketer will rejoice after finding out that the image creator and video uploader come standard with all pricing packages.

Empowered by Optimistic Philosophies – Sharing Encouraged

Listen to smart like-minded people. The thirst for knowledge should never end, and one of the best resources can be found and shared online. It is the outside-the-box thinking that drives industry professionals down the challenging yet fun road that can only be found in a startup environment.

True entrepreneurs not only rely, but feed off of those that share their same startup goals and principles. It's vital to every new brand to learn from the past and move forward in a new way. Here are a few social media content sharing and storytelling sites to learn, improve, and spark inspiration.

Hatch for Good

Read and learn from user generated stories and articles from businesses and consumers from a wide range of industries.

Sharing Encouraged: Want to share your own content, but don't know where to start? The content development guides will get your plan into motion and be sure to learn from a plethora of educational content related to social media engagement, strategy, and success evaluation.

Medium

Developed by tech mogul and Twitter co-founder Evan Williams, the sharing site is the ideal *medium* (pun intended) to read, learn, write, and interact with a community of online thought leaders.

Sharing Encouraged: Sign in and view stories written to and from users interested in anything from technology to sports – or write your own story and share it with the online community.

Slideshare

A LinkedIn company, Slideshare can build, upload, and edit presentation decks and share them on social media.

Sharing Encouraged: The list of sharing sites includes: Facebook, Twitter, Google+, and of course LinkedIn. Email, links, WordPress shortcodes, and iframe embedding also available.

Know When to Strike – A Constant Drive Led by Ambition

Harvey Mackay once said, "goals give you more than a reason to get up in the morning; they are an incentive to keep you going all day. Goals tend to tap the deeper resources and draw the best out of life." A constant yearning for excellence is a pivotal part of every startup enthusiast and what sets him or her apart from the pack.

Here are three must have tools to determine the effectiveness of your social media campaigns and strive to meet and exceed your digital goals.

Google Analytics

There's no doubt you know to some extent the incredible capabilities of Google Analytics. Measuring website traffic is key to mastering your audience and their behaviors. What you may not know is that Google Analytics is extremely useful to learning which social media network your visitors are coming from and what posts are encouraging interaction and clicks.

Driving Ambition: Google Analytics should be a standard portion of your review and social media assessment on a daily, weekly, or monthly basis. Google Analytics prides its platform on tracking goals. How can you ever set your own goals without the right infrastructure in place to track them?

Klout

Start by reviewing social media's most cravable content, and then track your audience's unique response to your posts.

Driving Ambition: The "Klout Score" reveals your brand's engagement from 0-100 on social media via retweets, likes, and shares. This score is perfect for setting a base metric and striving to reach new social media heights.

HowSociable

With close to 200,000 brand searches, HowSociable will measure the magnitude of your brand.

Driving Ambition: Historical data, social media mentions and metrics give you a better understanding of how your brand is performing on social media. Magnitude scoring is ranked from 0-10, with a score of zero representing little to no activity and a score of a ten for brands that are very active online.

Checking your brand score is as easy as typing in your name to the search bar – which begs the question, how sociable is your brand?

Always Changing, Always Adapting

Like your startup mentality, technology is always evolving to form the most up-to-date product and emerging vision. Remember that no matter what the size or age of your brand, when it comes to social media marketing, never forget the scrappy approach based on philosophies that drive you to reach your goals – to which is in essence the startup mentality.

Chapter 6

Stress and Strain Management

"Stress is an important dragon to slay - or at least tame - in your life."

-Marilu Henner

You are in a unique situation. Not only do you have to worry about the stressors that cause the rest of the population to loath five days of the week and live for two, you are also are trying to build a successful venture. Because of that truth, many part-time entrepreneurs' stress levels cause them to quit on their businesses prematurely. The key is to manage the stress and distress so that you can handle the unique challenges you will face as a part-time entrepreneur.

Human beings are inherently free, yet we keep finding countless ways to trap ourselves. In this day and age, it's easy to fall into the trap of social conditioning, and it is even easier to get caught up in work and everyday stress that the modern way of living inevitably brings.

We're overworked, overstressed, and sometimes, it feels like we're trying to find a way out of a maze that is our professional life. All of this can take a significant toll on one's health and well-being. It is a part of our heritage, tradition, and culture as entrepreneurs to be driven by our businesses. We want them to succeed so badly that we are sometimes willing to sacrifice our time, energy, relationships, and money for the realization of the vision we have for our businesses.

We can't help it, and many of us like it that way. We value the results of our hard work. But too often, we put "well-being" near the bottom of the to-do list. A study called, "Workaholism and Well-Being," conducted by the College of Human Ecology concluded that workaholism may have a severely negative effect on those who work long hours.

Researcher Sarah Asebedo said, "*We looked at the association between workaholism and physical and mental well-being. We found workaholics — defined by those working more than 50 hours per week — were more likely to have reduced physical well-being, measured by skipped meals. Also, we found that workaholism was associated with reduced mental well-being as measured by a self-reported depression score.*"

This is not good news. And the news doesn't get any better. Work addicts may be susceptible to multiple health issues including high blood pressure, fatigue, and stress. In Japan, overworking is responsible for an estimated 10,000 deaths of working men in the country each year, according to Japanese occupational health researchers. There is even a word for a death caused by working; karoshi.

There is something most workaholics have in common; they take themselves, their jobs, and their lives very seriously.

Entrepreneurs combat all of these issues we briefly reflected earlier in this article, on a daily basis. This poses a legitimate question: Is there a way to relieve stress in order to stay healthy, happy, and productive while constantly working hard? Luckily, there are quite a few ways, but here we will focus on seven things most of us can take the time to do. They are, as follows:

• Meditation

• Exercise

• Presence

• Regular Relaxation

• Laughter

Now, let's break it down even further and talk a bit about each of these fice equally important techniques if you will, that work together in synergy and have the power to help every workaholic out there.

Healthy Habits are the First to Go; Maintain Them

It is a well-known fact that physical activity helps release feel-good hormones, but regular exercise significantly reduces stress. Even if you're a true workaholic, taking the time to exercise regularly (at least a few times a week) is something that you can do and, most definitely, the best possible thing you can do for yourself. There is an old Latin saying that goes: "In a healthy body, a healthy mind," and it conceptually summarizes the core essence and purpose of regular physical activity.

Resting Better

At times, your business might require more hours from you than you may have readily available. In these cases, the rest that you do get daily should be quality rest. To make sure that the rest you are getting is enough to give you the mental and physical recovery you need, you to make sure that you are resting better. A key to making this habit work is unplugging 45 minutes to an hour before bedtime.

Try silent meditation or reading before bed, instead of checking Email or watching TV. The second key is actually getting up when your alarm goes off. No matter how groggy you may feel, forcing those next thirty minutes of alarm interrupted sleep will cut into your preparation time and leave you less time to really wake up.

In an interview with Inc.com, the CEO of PEX card stated "I've learned that I can be much more productive if I wake up early, between 4:45 and 5:30 a.m. and get one to two hours of solid work done before my family starts their day. It also makes me happy that I'm reserving time for my wife and girls at the end of the day. All in all, this is a well-balanced work-life system." Adjust your daily routine to fit with a calm productive morning, and the rest of your day will feel far less stressful.

Keep moving

It's no secret that exercise is important. We see it in magazines, on Instagram, and hear about it at every doctor's appointment. Fortunately, regular exercise doesn't mean learning to lift at a gym or running a 5k. Something as simple as taking a walk during your lunch break or trying yoga in the morning can leave you feeling more refreshed throughout the day.

Exercise is attributed to extra endorphins (a better attitude), and self-confidence (a better self-image), both of which can help you shine during meetings and make you far more open to connecting with coworkers and clients. A study by the Montreal Heart Institute also suggests that physical activity can make you more creative and improve cognitive function, all of which can be beneficial to a business owner.

"In a new study, previously sedentary adults were put through four months of high-intensity interval training. At the end, their cognitive functions – the ability to think, recall and make quick decisions – had improved significantly," says Dr. Martin Juneau, director of prevention at the Montreal Heart Institute. "If you talk to people who exercise, they say they feel sharper. Now we've found a way to measure that." Find the exercise schedule that works best for you, and be sure to stick to it.

Regular Relaxation Habit

Relaxation is something every entrepreneur should consider making an integral part of their life. All of these techniques we've talked about are incredibly useful and complement each other wonderfully, but doing them on and off, from time to time and "when you feel like it" won't do much to permanently calm and relax that inner workaholic.

Every workaholic, every entrepreneur, every student should try and make relaxation a habit. If you are a true part-time entrepreneur, you probably have a pretty busy schedule that you tend to religiously stick to, but taking 10 minutes each day, for a start, is definitely something you can do.

Take Some Time Off, For Crying Out Loud

Deadlines, debts, bills, business ideas that never work, unreliable coworkers, market trends and changes – all of these things are something every entrepreneur faces on a daily, if not hourly, basis. There is indeed a way to cope with all of that built up stress. All that it takes is some dedication.

On those insane days full of extensive projects or back-to-back meetings, you may think that the best thing is to rush from task to task and then force yourself to work on your business once you arrive home in the evening. A far better plan is to allow yourself short 5 to 10 minute breaks a few times a day, even if this means excusing yourself to the bathroom or faking an important phone call.

Use these breaks as a chance to try deep breathing exercises, listen to one of your mood enhancing playlists, or have a brief chat with a friend who cheers you up. Breaks can actually increase your energy and morale, and make you more productive as the day goes on. Try not to schedule yourself back to back.

For example, if you have a two-hour break between job one and your part-time business, try not to fill it with doctor's appointments and errands. Instead, go for a nice walk or sit in a favorite café and enjoy a cup of coffee. Hard work is important, but no one will benefit from you running yourself into the ground.

As you embark on your next busy week or hectic day, try using some of these tips to help lighten the load and improve your mood. You may find it easier to keep up with the grind after allowing yourself the time and space to take care of other needs outside of work. Mental and physical rest is important, even on those weeks where the "grind" doesn't seem to stop.

Have Downtime

Lots of people attribute success to drive, drive, drive- the constant push towards the next big project and the next big idea. While ambition is important, it is equally important to know the value of downtime. Giving yourself an hour of "me" time each day can help calm stress, stimulate creativity, and give you an overall more positive attitude.

Take solo lunches and read a favorite book, or wake up an hour early and enjoy your favorite guilty pleasure TV show. You can also try meditation, yoga, or taking long strolls. All of these activities promote mental clarity and keep stress at bay. No one advocates laziness, but treating yourself to a private hour during the day can make the rest of the day feel less overwhelming.

Another idea is taking a vacation once a month. This isn't to say pack up and book a hotel room for yourself, but giving yourself a Saturday a month for favorite activities can keep you in high spirits. Go out with friends, do some shopping, or spend all day in your PJ's drinking wine- whatever it takes to get you feeling relaxed and ready to face that next big thing head on.

Adding these healthy habits into your life can keep the energy high, the stress low, and the ideas flowing.

Chapter 7

Creating Time from Thin Air

If you are the only person among your coworkers, family members, or friends that has started a part-time business, congratulations. This means despite many of the obstacles that make it difficult to operate an extremely successful business you decided to take the plunge.

Even though your friends, family, and coworkers think it is cool that you started your own business, they have undoubted told you why they would never be able to do it even though they've thought about it. Of all of the excuses you will hear, "not enough time" will often top the list. Now, if you ask us, not having enough time is not a valid reason for not pursuing the life you want. However, we will admit that running a business while working a full-time job does take some unique time management practices.

Your commitment to your job may not affect your commitment to your business, but it will affect how much time you can spend on it. There is no way to finagle your way to getting more time. You have 24 hours like everyone else. You will need to be smart and conscious of how you spend your seconds.

Because you have a job, you have limited hours. In a sense, your efficiency as a part-time entrepreneur is even more important than a full-time entrepreneur's. The reason is the fact that you will have less time to do more.

In this chapter, we are going to show you how to get the most out of the two most important times of the day; nights and mornings. For the majority of part-time entrepreneurs, this is the only time they can work on their business without getting fired from their job.

Making the Most of Mornings

Productivity is an integral thing. Ask any worker around what the most challenging aspect of their job is. Chances are a majority will list lack of productivity as a real deal-breaker. It takes so much effort for them to be productive, especially at the start of the day. Entrepreneurs also suffer from the funk, just like the "regular" people.

But fret not, for there are ways that can make productivity a truly natural thing for entrepreneurs. There's no big secret here, just some simple common sense tips to fire up your neurons in the morning and let you make the most of your early hours. Here are some of the tips:

A Natural Head Start.

Remember Richard Branson, someone who launched what seems like hundreds of companies in the span of 40 short business years? Do you know what lifestyle habit he follows? His day starts at 5 a.m. in the morning. Every day, he wakes up at that time. But how does that help him? And more significantly, how would it help you?

1. It gives you ample time to collect your focus, far from the noise and the humdrum of the daily life. In short, it gives you time to get your mind ready.

2. When you wake up early and you give your mind the time to collect its focus properly, you will observe that your mind is armed with discipline. This discipline is reflected in the actions you take, such as when you get out of bed BEFORE you even get out of it. You visualize everything beforehand, making your action happen earlier than you do so.

3. You cut through the crap, making less choices but significant choices that get things done. You don't devote your energies to anything or any thought that may distract you from your goal(s), no matter how mundane or

frivolous those choices seem to be. You save your mind's energy for what matters.

Now, when you combine clear focus with steely mindful discipline, you are able to do a lot more in the formative morning hours than in the whole day put together. In short, your productivity gets a supercharged boost. Instead of devoting too much time (and energy) to things like what to have for breakfast or what to wear to the office, you can think about accomplishing the goals you have set for yourself. You are, in essence, simplifying your decision-making process by automating most of the insignificant ones.

Managing Energy; Not time

In the bestselling book "The Power of Full Engagement" authors Jim Loehr and Tony Schwartz emphasis the importance of managing your energy instead of your time. This works especially well for morning productivity. There may be certain things that you can do better in the mornings.

Some people lose some of their creative energy as the day goes on. Things like email, meetings, and operational tasks, can cause a person's creativity to nap. If you are one of those types of individuals, try to use your time in the morning to nurture your creativity.

Maybe the mornings could be the time when you brainstorm new ideas, develop new marketing strategies, or find new ways to grow your business. It may be harder to do at the end of the day when you've been working on so many other things.

The same could be said about the right time for personal growth. Many, many successful entrepreneurs and CEOs use mornings to read, exercise, pray, or spend time working towards completing a personal achievement (i.e., train for a marathon). We've said it many times on StartUp Mindset, your business will only grow as much as you will. Take time in the mornings before the busyness of the day begins to do something that will bring you personal satisfaction and that will also help you grow as an individual.

In her book What the Most Successful People Do Before Breakfast-A Short Guide to Making Over Your Morning, Laura Vanderkam outlines a few things successful people routinely do to start their mornings. It seems that habit formation is essential for a productive morning. Trying to revamp your entire morning by redoing every bad habit is a doomed mission.

The most effective way to change your morning habits is to change one habit at a time. That habit will eventually turn into a part of your morning ritual and thus create the opportunity to introduce a new habit.

These tips are enough to help the most forward-thinking entrepreneurs make the most of their day and that too just by waking up early in the morning. Waking up early is great for the grey matter cells, and it only bodes well for making decisions that can significantly impact the direction of your business.

The Night Shift: Making the Most of Your Nights

We are all different, and our minds and bodies function differently. The terms "early bird" and "night owl" are not mere societal constructs or urban myths – essentially, you are either a morning or a night person and there is science to back up these claims (we will elaborate further on that below). An early bird is someone who feels alert, awake, and productive early in the morning, while a night owl can be considered someone who functions best during the night and goes to sleep late. The point is – some of us are simply predisposed to work and operate at night.

Getting the most from the graveyard shift

There is a certain prejudice that those who get up early get the job done and night owls simply don't get enough credit. If you sleep in, people think you're just being lazy. However, according to a recent scientific study, conducted at the London School of Economics and Political Science, it's actually the other way around. In fact, the same study found that there is a link between high cognitive complexity and staying up late.

This poses a set of legitimate questions, with the most important one being: how to be a productive night owl? While night owls experience high mental activity late at night, that doesn't mean they channel that mental energy properly. Channeling and making use of that mental clarity, energy, and focus and turning it into creation and productivity is a challenge in itself, but there are some things each and every night owl can do to be highly productive. Below are some helpful tips and tricks, listed in no particular order.

Stick to the Schedule

Having a regular wake-up time is absolutely crucial. The body gets used to a certain rhythm, and in order for it to function like a well-oiled clock, waking up around the same time every day is a must. A lot of night owls tend to oversleep and therefore, unknowingly, set an elaborate trap for themselves. Sleeping too much doesn't lead to productivity; it can actually lead to lethargy.

According to Medical Daily, by sleeping longer than normal, we unknowingly throw off our regular circadian rhythm-a 24-hour cycle that is driven by our biological clocks and results in physical, mental, and behavioral changes. Simply put, if you want to be a productive night owl – stick to a schedule.

Night owls have the ability to completely immerse themselves in mentally challenging work at night, but this can sometimes be counterproductive. A study at the University of Liege in Belgium, for example, found that night owls are much more capable of working long hours than early birds.

This essentially means that night owls are more likely to be workaholics and to work non-stop without taking breaks. On the other hand, taking relatively frequent, short breaks can do wonders for one's productivity. Relax, get some fresh air, walk around the room, play some music – whatever does the trick.

Channel Your Inner Vampire

If you're a person who thinks nighttime is the best time to get things done, chances are, you've watched the sun come up as you work, countless times. While you may shrug this off as typical for a night owl, the National Sleep Foundation reports that quality of sleep and light exposure are very much related and dependent on each other. Our bodies and minds are not used to so much light and, even if you are able to fall asleep easily when the sun is up, consider going to bed while it's still dark outside. This will improve the quality of your sleep and, in return, make you more productive the next day. If it ever happens that you're up until the morning, consider darkening your windows completely before you go to bed.

Also, in order to ensure that your sleep is sound enough, be sure to not go directly to bed after you finish working. The main reason for this is to allow yourself time to wind-down. The ability you have to relax before you rest may affect the quality of rest. Making sure you rest well is vital to your performance.

Create a Power Playlist

Most people who run or workout consistently will most likely tell you that they have a specific set of songs on their iPod or phone that they listen to while working out. The reason for this is to have some motivation and distraction for doing a tough task.

I often wonder why more offices don't use this approach. Teresa Lesiuk, an assistant professor in the music therapy program at the University of Miami, has studied the effect music has on productivity. In one study, she found that those who listened to music completed their tasks more quickly and came up with better ideas than those who didn't. Music improves mood, and mood seems to affect productivity. "It breaks you out of just thinking one way," Lesiuk says.

Use background music as a pacesetter for your nighttime work. It may ward off sleepiness as well as improve your performance.

The Bottom Line: Pay Attention to Yourself and Your Environment

Productivity depends on both the inner and the outer world. Listen to your mind and your body, adjust your schedule to your internal clock and, at the same time, try to pay attention to your surroundings and working environment. Adjust and adapt everything to yourself in order to create the perfect ambience for productivity and in order to become what you have the power to be – a productive night owl, not a slacker who sleeps in and procrastinates.

Removing Distractions

You have a ton of things to do but for some reason, you are fascinated by what people are posting on Instagram, where your friends are eating dinner, and the latest rant from @KimKardasian on Twitter.

You know there has to be a better way to spend your free time, but you cannot seem to stop yourself from being distracted. Our easy access to information and entertainment has made it hard for us to focus on other things. This section is designed to help you limit or completely eliminate the digital distractions in your life. Many of these tips will not only limit how much you are online, but will help you stay focused on the tasks at hand.

Go Back in Time (FREEDOM)

Freedom is an great app that locks you away from the Internet so that you can focus on other things. Freedom is good because it allows you to travel back in time before all of the digital distractions existed. Without the constant temptation of checking email or browsing YouTube, you will be forced to do something more productive with your time.

The best way to utilize your time in the dark ages is to schedule what you are going to do with your new found freedom. For example, if you decided that you would like two hours a night of freedom from the Internet, plan what you will do with that time before you unplug from the net.

Unplug the Net (Net Nanny)

What happens if you need to use the Internet but you want to use the Internet for projects, homework, or other things, but you don't want to get sucked up into an Internet journey? In this case, software that limits the Internet instead of completely eliminating it works best. Then you may want to use a content filtering software like Net Nanny.

Net Nanny is an Internet content filter used by parents to prevent their little ones from stumbling onto something inappropriate for them. The software is still pretty awesome for getting rid of distracting content of all kinds.

Think about the types of websites that distract you the most or that you would like to visit less. If it seems like you click on every Miley Cyrus drug use article that you come across, then using a new blocking tool that will filter that or similar content will be your best bet to kick that habit. Block those sites and keywords that tend to lure you away from doing what you want.

Rescue Time

You may be an Internet addict and not even know it. In order to know know what really distracts you, you will need to know how you spend your time online. Download a software program that will track your Internet usage and offers reports for how you spend your time. A tool like Rescue Time can help show you the truth of how you spend your time. Rescue Time has an option of tracking and creating reports of what sites you use and how much time you spent on social media, email, and other sites.

Similar to Net Nanny, there is an option to block certain sites that may distract you as well.

Some of these types of these content filtering software have a mobile version. To be sure that you have no distractions around you, download a version for every device that may steal your attention.

Give Up Your Passcode

Your phone may be the major culprit that steals the majority of your time. To prevent yourself from constantly grabbing your phone and playing Candy Crush or checking Facebook, hand your phone over to someone you trust and allow them to set the pass code to unlock your phone.

Since the pass code doesn't prevent phones from receiving calls, you can still answer the phone if someone you need to talk to calls. But, since you don't have the code, you will be prevented from making calls out to anyone just to chat.

Ignore all Requests and Eliminate the Unnecessary

Besides friend requests and some (but very few) requests to like a page, I never accept any request. Not game requests, or any other application request. The reason for this is to keep my personal Facebook page as basic as possible. The less access I have to games and tools, the less time I will spend on Facebook.

I also limit how many apps are on my phone. As soon as I get a new phone, I browse through the apps that are already installed. Apps that I know I will never use get deleted. It turns out that many of the apps do similar things or the exact same thing. For example, my previous Android phone was equipped with Maps, Google Maps, and TeleNavigation, which are all GPS applications. It also had FM radio, Play Music, and Slacker Radio. And then it had Play Magazines and Zinio (magazine app). My goal was to clean out all of the apps that I don't use and only download the few that I use.

Using DuckDuckGo and Google Instead of Yahoo and Bing

Nothing against Yahoo but their homepage is a huge conglomerate distraction for the eyes. Trending topics, "news" stories, sports scores, and other flashy things are designed to keep your eyes on their site. I have an email address there which I have decided to only check on my phone because of the distractions Yahoo presents. Don't get me wrong, I'm sure the story about Jwwwo and Snooki's photo shoot is interesting, but you've got more important things to do. Bing search engine often flashes distracting news stories as well.

Google isn't perfect, those Google doodles can sometimes throw a person off track, but you're much more likely to get back to doing what you were doing once you've played the digital guitar. If you still think that Google will be a distraction, Duckduckgo.com is a search engine that is becoming one of my favorites.

Purge Your Subscriptions

The average Internet user spends 19% of their time online on email and communication. I absolutely believe this statistic and I probably exceed that number. Just going through one of my personal email addresses at Yahoo this week, I found there were only four relevant emails. The rest were updates and deals from stores, a few restaurants, some e-bills, and about nine of them were from Yahoo. This is too much. I need my life back, and purging many of my subscriptions will help me do that.

Find all of the emails subscriptions that are not useful and eliminate the spammers. Keep the blogs you read (such as StartUp Mindset) and other sites that add value to your life instead of taking time away from it.

Turn Notifications OFF

You can also turn off text notifications so that you are not notified when a text message comes in. This will prevent you from checking your phone and breaking your focus when someone texts you.

Use "StayFocusd"

Stayfocusd is a Google Chrome extension that limits that amount of time you can spend on particular sites. If you are working on a project and want to eliminate all distractions for a certain period of time, this extension will allow you to do just that.

Chapter 8

The Idea

"Whatever you want in life, other people are going to want it too. Believe in yourself enough to accept the idea that you have an equal right to it."

-Diane Sawyer

Coming up with ideas

Anytime is a great time to gear up and start a business. To start a business, you, of course, need to come up with a great winning idea. Business startup ideas can be gotten from anywhere and at any time. Stephen Key, the author of "One Simple Idea for Startups and Entrepreneurs: Live Your Dreams and Create Your Own Profitable Company" (McGrawHill, 2012) and co-founder of inventright.com based in Glenbrook, says he generates ideas by finding several ways to engage his mind, from walking the aisles of stores to brainstorming about the openings in the marketplace.

An idea can suddenly come up in your mind and be a killer idea; however, there are many techniques that can be employed to get your creative juices flowing and ensure that you come up with an amazing business idea; To develop a great business idea, ask yourself, "What's next?" A lot of successful business ideas are usually ahead of the curve. Do not think of present technologies only, the field has already been oversaturated. Think about trends and technologies on the horizon and about how you might make a move into those areas.

An example is the hoverboards that are the wave now. Think about what services you can offer to owners of this and when it does get very popular like a car is, what you can offer to owners of this new generation gadget. Another example is the innovations regarding the home entertainment systems that Apple and other companies are developing; they are developing new entertainment technologies, think about these technologies and in what ways you can provide services to owners of these new technologies. Developing an idea this way is great as when the new technologies do come around, your business would already be prepared to cater to the needs of users of these new technologies.

If it bugs you, it's probably bugging other humans. Do something about what bugs you. Is there something that bugs you so much and keeps you wishing there was a way to make the procedure simpler and easier? The odds are that you are not the only one being bugged by it. Think about what bugs you to no end, and build your business around the solution to that thing. If it bugs you that it takes too long to get a car, open a company where getting a car is a breeze. People would flock to your business and get cars far faster than usual, and you'll make profits in bunches.

If it bugs you that the procedure to get something is too long or hard, build a business that takes a little of that stress and waiting time away, and sit and watch your business flourish. Colin Barceloux, the founder of Bookrenter.com, a business that offers textbook rentals at about 60% discount, was bothered by just how costly a textbook was. He took a move to fix that and opened his business in 2007. What began as a one-man business opened out of frustration now has more than two million users and hundreds of employees and has helped students save more than $240,000,000. As Barceloux puts it, "You just have to look at what frustrates you; There is your business idea right there." Do not reinvent the wheel; Look for new niches. While developing an idea, do not necessarily do what Mr. A and Mrs. B have done and have prospered, your business idea does not have to reinvent the wheel. Sit back, take a look at what the masses would love to have but the big players in the industry are overlooking and figure out how you can fulfill that need.

A perfect example of someone who developed a business idea to fill the gap is the owner of Hot Picks. He started his company after realizing the fact that major brands in the guitar pick industry were offering only conventional picks and no novelty picks. He began with a skull-shaped pick that was sold in about 1,000 stores, including 7-Eleven and Wal-Mart.

Today, he is among the big companies in the guitar pick world and offers thousands of different shapes and designs of novelty guitar picks. Look for a need that is being ignored by the big corporations and create a business to fill that. In the same vein as the last chapter, I end this with the words of Key, the founder of Hot Picks "The big guys leave a tremendous amount of opportunity on the table," Create a cheaper version of an existing product. If you do not see an area left neglected by the bigger brands, and so cannot open a business focusing on a new niche, you can open a company that offers what the larger companies offer, at a cheaper price. A lot of new businesses start out this way, by offering customers another version of an existing product at a lower price.

Now, a very crucial thing to note here is not to cut down on the essential part of the product you'll be offering at a lower price. Say, if it's a prescription glass business you are founding, you can save costs on the frames and not use a premium frame that would last thousands of years and not be scratched (many buyers do not care for this, and nobody lives for thousands of years) and rather invest in a frame that would at least be durable, and then offer a cheaper product. Most times, you might not even need to offer a quality in any way less than the already established company's own. Most companies try to make about 50% profits on each sale, as a new business, you can aim to make 20%, and you'll surely get your customers.

Warby Parker is an eyeglasses company launched in 2010 by four business school friends. Prescription glasses are sold at about $300 or more; they offered them at $95 and have since grown into a force to be reckoned with. Find a category lacking recent innovations. Another way to come up with a great business idea is to identify areas in the market that have not had any innovations recently and try to provide that. Talk to your prospective customers.

The aim of starting a business is to make money. This is done by meeting the needs of people and getting paid for it, If all the tips above fail to help you come up with a great idea, you can take the most direct route of all and directly talk to shoppers. They are the ones whose needs you are trying to meet, so there is no better way to come up with an idea than by talking to them. If you are interested in video games, hang out in the aisles of video game shops and ask customers what they think is missing and wish they could find in the marketplace or send out online surveys to the relevant sites and learn about their needs. This is actually one of the best ways to come up with a business idea. You already have people wanting this, so give it to them and have a successful business.

Cultivating Innovation

Innovation is not a personality trait most are born with, it needs to be cultivated through practice. By opening your mind and thinking differently, you come up with ideas that maybe nobody has thought of before. You may even become a pioneer in your field when you master innovation. How important is this for business growth? You have the potential to stand out in front of your competitors. Your business could grow exponentially with just one great idea. So how do you think outside of the box and find that game changing idea that will boost your business? Here are some ways to push your mind into finding new ideas.

Challenge Your Usual Mental Thoughts

To break free from stagnation, you must first address what you're thinking. When you challenge your assumptions, you can start to consider possibilities you wouldn't have before. If you see yourself as not having enough money to start an online campaign, you don't get the growth from that area of marketing. To get the money, you could work overtime, sell some things out of the garage you don't use, or dip into savings.

You can also state the problem in a different way than you normally would. By rewording the roadblock or problem, you may see it differently. Consider what would happen if you don't solve the problem or ask yourself why the problem should be solved. Tackling the issue differently in your mind can open up new insights. You may come up with entirely different solutions to obstacles by simply asking different questions.

Express Yourself Differently

If you're used to typing ideas into a Word document, you may not be utilizing your mind's creativity. According to a study from Princeton University, students who wrote with pen to paper have a greater expansion for learning than those who used a notebook to type. Taking this further, if you expressed ideas through drawing, painting, or writing a song, you may conjure something great up from your creative mind. You can tap into potential ideas that are currently out of reach by doing something out of your comfort zone. Have yourself an artistic afternoon, and you never know what interesting innovations can be conjured up.

Change Your Perspective

Your perspective, if left unchanged, will yield the same type of ideas every time. This doesn't allow for the growth and change you're hoping for. One of the ways to gain a different perspective is to talk with someone else. Ask a few people what they would do in your situation. Talk with friends or colleagues that are all in different professions. People who were brought up in a different culture may have totally different views that could be a game changer to your whole industry.

Another way to get a different perspective is to put yourself in someone else's shoes. If you have a mentor within your industry, consider what they would do in your situation. The closer you follow that person, the more you'll know about their activity. The concept here is to identify with their traits and use them to seek out solutions. So, if you're thinking Richard Branson, you might bring in traits such as risk taking, big thinking, and flashy advertising.

Be Aware at All Times

You've probably seen a crime story at one point where the

detective is struggling with a mystery. He finds the missing puzzle piece while relaxing at a coffee shop. The coffee cup that inspires him is the key to the case because he's reminded of a second coffee cup found at the murder scene. This also applies to innovative ideas. Many of the most brilliant ideas occurred from "happy accidents" during times you aren't focused on solutions. Innovation is less of a systematic method and is connected to the creative mind so ideas come sporadically and usually from left field.

Of course, it's important to brainstorm, as the "happy accident" is a result of putting many things into your conscious. It is said that innovative ideas are always going to have an element of serendipity to them. Pay attention to where possibilities reveal themselves. Real life situations such as a mother struggling in the park with her dog and baby stroller. If you're in the industry, you may realize there should be a solution for this problem. If you sell services online, check out forums within your industry and see what people are crying out for.

Supportive Practices

Innovative ideas need a solid foundation based on positivity and other enablers. Maintaining practices that nurture your mind will enhance your ability to come up with incredible ideas. Here are some practices that can promote creativity within;

- Have faith in yourself, and believe that ideas will come. These kind of pep talks with yourself will allow you to perform better.

- Maintain a healthy lifestyle that includes things which make you feel good. This can range from listening to music, playing with your kids, napping, or taking a walk. You may think that working hard will benefit you. The brain breaks are probably more beneficial and often as you are in play time, the big ideas will come to you then.

- Change your settings from time to time. If you work from home, go work at a coffee shop. If you're working in an office, brainstorming might work better away from your desk. Have a meeting outside in the park instead of a stuffy boardroom.

- De-clutter your life. Clean out your closets and keep them organized. Do the same in every space of your home and office.

- When you work, turn off your phone and only check in on things at specific times you've set. Brainstorming for ideas should be distraction free.

In order to maximize business growth, new ideas are essential. By practicing techniques that force the mind to think out of the box, you can acquire the skill of innovative thinking. By daily creating a positive atmosphere through the practices above, you allow space for creativity. Creativity is at the core of innovation. Another foundation of innovation is knowledge. You have to have an expert knowledge in your field. Know what people want, know the limitations, and the tone to present your innovative ideas.

Testing Your Ideas

Before you go ahead to actually start your business, there are ways to test your idea to see if it is capable of really making you money or not. Somewhere between scribbling your idea on a piece of paper and starting a business, there is a process you need to carry out that mainly determines either your success or failure in business. A lot of times, would-be entrepreneurs get carried away by their "epiphanies," the moments they imagine they have found the perfect idea and forget to test the idea to find out if it is actually viable or not. There are some steps required to test your business idea; these steps are necessary so as to keep from wasting valuable time and money on unfocused or untargeted activities.

Of course, there are times that an idea turns out to be a great business idea anyways, in spite of a lack of market research. Unfortunately, a lot of other occasions, an untested idea always crashes and burns. Note down your ideas and expand them This is the very next step after deciding on an idea, you have identified the areas and needs that you want your business to improve upon. The next step is to try to and expand on this, Write out your idea, and see where it can be developed.

Sit down and study your chosen idea thoroughly, making sure nothing is being left unconsidered. Carrying out a Competitive Analysis is an excellent way to compare and predict just how well your business will stand up against your competition in the industry. There are many steps involved in carrying out a competitive analysis; they are arranged below. Model your business. If your idea for a business seems too tiresome and clunky, it is great to create a model for it.

It's not only when the idea feels clunky that a model is needed. Creating a model is very easy to do, and updating it is a breeze.

With a model, you get to enjoy a clear overview of the building blocks of your business idea: the customer segments, channels to reach out to clients, value propositions, revenue streams, key resources, customer relationships, principal partners, activities that create value, and cost structures.

Execute a market survey. After a model has been created, the next step in testing your business idea is to execute a market survey. A Market Survey is an organized effort to gather information about your target audience or customers. Absolutely no business should be launched without the execution of a market survey. A market survey provides important information to identify and analyze the market need, market size, and your competition.

There are sites where this can be done, you just create an online questionnaire and share the link to the survey with your target audience. This transcends geographic boundaries, and helps you gain a broader, global perspective and is often more preferred to the traditional method of printing out and handing questionnaires yourself, although a combination of both is the best approach.

Another way of carrying out a market survey is to conduct a Focus Group Session both before and after the completion of your Minimum Viable Product. Here, you invite people from your chosen target demographic to participate in a group discussion on the products or services. They would be advised to speak freely about what they want done; that is before the product is ready and what they want to be changed, when it is done. A focus group is a very good idea, and would help achieve the following:

• It helps you find out your customer's first impression of the product.

• It helps gather real-time customer's feedback on the virtues and vices of the products.

• When that is done, you can now tweak and improve your product before it is finally deliverable (launched).

After Testing Your Idea

After testing your idea, like all tests, there would be one of two outcomes. first, it might turn out that your idea is a great one or the test might reveal your idea to be a flop. No matter what the outcome is, the steps below should guide your next line of action.

When Your Idea Looks Like a Flop

If when your idea is tested, you discover a lot of holes in it, it doesn't mean you need to totally scrap the whole business start-up plan and resign yourself to life as an employee. Sometimes, the "terrible" idea is just in need of some reworking. It can be disheartening when an idea is revealed to be a flop, considering the amount of time and money you have already invested in it, first during the idea stage, and then the market research stage to test it. However, giving up is never and has never been the right option.

Rather, it is recommended that you take time out and focus your energy on determining exactly why your idea would not work and where it needs improvements to ensure future success. Although no entrepreneur wants to hear that his "idea" is flawed, only by listening and reacting to feedback from others can he give his idea a chance for success.

Ask yourself, is the weakness one that can be overcome? If the answer is yes, work on overcoming it. However, if your answer is no and the weakness discovered in your plan cannot be overcome and the idea made to create true value for your customer and your business, it is time to leave that idea and pursue another one. Remember again that a lot of ideas simply need some fine-tuning; before giving up on one, closely consider if you can make the idea work. After all, there was a reason you thought of that idea in the first place. Now for the other option after testing.

Your Idea is Great and Ready to Go

If your idea has stood the test of the market research you've conducted, then it is time to progress to the next level, releasing your goods/services to the public. A very key factor to consider is pricing, you want to set a price that is competitive and still capable of influencing people's decision to buy from you. This is especially necessary if there is much competition. The beauty of setting your price is that you have the option to change it at will if the pricing structure isn't working. A tip to setting a price: your services/product is to always start high, now, do not immediately dismiss this advice, think about it.

When you start high, and the pricing structure isn't working, you can go a tad lower, your customers would be happy that your product is now "cheaper" and they'll purchase more from you. If however you start low, you can never go up without losing a lot of customers who will feel your services are too "costly." It is best to test different pricing offers, each month, set a new price for your services, and remember to keep going a little bit lower until you reach the minimum percentage of profit you have decided to make on each product.

Another very important tip when your idea is ready to go is to be sure you are selling your products/services where your target market is likely to buy. Your marketing plan and budget should include a well-crafted distribution strategy. If you have decided to sell over the Internet, set a budget for media fees to drive new customers to your site. If you want to sell via retail distribution, you might need workers with industry experience to help you reach your target market.

Chapter 9

The Money

"Here's how I think of my money - as soldiers - I send them out to war everyday. I want them to take prisoners and come home, so there's more of them."

-Kevin O'Leary

One of the issues that many aspiring entrepreneurs struggle with is money. This is understandable, because many full-time and seasoned entrepreneurs have the same issue. Managing the money you make, no matter how small to start, will be vital to your success.

Running your business part-time gives you the opportunity to avoid many of the mistakes entrepreneurs make with money. Because you will be starting up, you can build good money management habits that will make it easier for you to improve efficiency, increase profits, and minimize losses as your business starts to grow.

Funding

Convincing people about the viability and awesomeness of your personal this-is-it moment can wait, raising funding for your startup cannot. After all, someone needs to fuel up this thing before it can gain traction and admirers in the industry. So, let's take a look at the hardest step in launching your startup from the ground. Not a simple undertaking admittedly, but with the right person, the right investors, and the right confidence, closing the deal is possible.

Using Personal Funds

The first question you need to ask yourself before putting your own cash into your business is "can I afford it?" You need think carefully about how much money you will need for initial capital and working capital. Starting and running a business is often costlier than most entrepreneurs think (more on that later). You want to ensure that you put enough money into your business, but also hold onto enough personal assets for a emergencies.

Personal funds can include bank accounts, credit cards and lines of credit, investment accounts, and retirement accounts. When using credit cards and lines of credit, be sure that you are using the lowest interest rate credit line available to you. Most credit cards have interest rates ranging from 8%-24%. This makes it a relatively low cost option if you decide to borrow. Ideally, when using personal funds, you want to use the option that costs you the least.

In the beginning, you'll spend more money than you make.

For some people, the idea of entrepreneurship means raking in the dough and being in charge of how much money they'd like to earn. Consistent and diligent entrepreneurship *leads* to this ideal, but it certainly doesn't *start* with it.

Again, there's no magic formula that suggests that if you spend X amount of money, you'll earn Y amount of money in Z time. In fact, getting a return on your investment is a bonus in entrepreneurship, because there's no real way to guarantee that what you're doing will actually pay off.

Family and Friends

Consider your friends and family as the people who can help you secure your first round of funding. This can give you enough leeway to create value around your idea and hopefully catch the eye of the people in the industry.

Be advised though that more often than not, startups can't even take off. It's just what it is. **There is always the risk of jeopardizing your family's money and friendships in the process**. So, when looking for funding from friends and family, determine if they are in a position to afford to lose it. For the sake of the relationship, YOU will have to determine if they can afford it, not them.

Just because your aunt Mary believes she can give you $5,000 from her savings account because she gets Social Security each month, doesn't mean she can actually afford to lose that money. Tread carefully and as a courtesy, be sure to warn them upfront about the risks associated with this venture.

Before taking cash from family and friends, you may want to run what Ed Zimmerman, co-founder of VentureCrush, calls "The Thanksgiving Litmas Test."

"*If you took money from friends or family and that would make a subsequent Thanksgiving dinner really suck, don't do it.*" *If you believe that it will in any meaningful way negatively alter the dynamics in the relationship, then think really hard and shy away from doing it,*" Zimmerman writes in one of his Wallstreet Journal "The Accelerators" articles.

Convertible Debt

One method that has proven to be immensely popular in recent years is that of convertible debt. Incubators like Y Combinator are known to secure at least $150,000 in convertible debts for every startup that qualifies for them. In layman's term, a convertible debt can be turned into liquid equity in the future, subject to certain goals and milestones your startup achieves. That's like having another round of funding waiting for you.

Startup Competitions

Startup competitions are good for realizing your dreams. Even though you might not manage to win the competition and secure funding, the truth is that getting into one can prove to be a treasure trove of opportunities and networking.

You can get in touch with many resources who believe in your idea as much as you do. That being said, there are no dearth of opportunities for startups to secure funding via a spate of major competitions. We have listed nine of them below who offer nothing less than $3 million to help you get on the road to success. Your part-time business may not qualify to win some of these competitions, but they are worth looking into.

1. Huggies Mom Inspired Grant Program

You know Huggies, the popular diaper company? It turns out that they have a yearly program that funds startups that have ideas of particular interest to moms. Their judges value creativity behind your idea and as long as it's relevant to motherhood, Huggies will have no issue green lighting it. Applicants should be over 21 years of age.

Prize: $15,000 of seed money.

2. Y Combinator Winter Funding

Y Combinator is one of the best ventures for funding startups. They select startups that are in their infancy, providing them invaluable support via investor meetings, networking, and more. Every startup is vetted by an experienced group of investors and venture capitalists.

Prize: $20,000

3. N.Y.C. Next Idea Competition

This competition is open to teams from all over the world. They are always on the lookout for new and unique business ideas that can be launched in N.Y.C. The startups are judged by a panel of investors based in New York. Teams can have two to five members. It is only open to students and alumni who have graduated from an institution of higher education.

Prize: $35,000

4. Institute for Entrepreneurial Leadership Annual Business Plan Competition

This competition is held primarily to help guide you through the whole process of developing a business plan from an idea to an actionable course or plan. Eligibility is based on a startup's understanding of the prevailing market conditions, growth options, and sustainable planning.

It's about helping learn the benefits of competitive advantage, thanks to skill sets and management methods that deliver. It's also about formulating a long-term vision and clearly-defined goals. The program is open only to for-profit entities and funds startups willing to set up shop in New Jersey.

Prize: Free IFEL Accelerator membership for 1 year and numerous cash prizes worth thousands of dollars.

5. Green Idea Factory Annual Competition

Like its name, the competition only caters to startups that can help in the aspects of recycling, entrepreneurship, green industries, and renewable energy. It is open only to local high schools.

Prize: $7,000

6. Hatch Pitch

Are you a startup that believes in making life better? Then Hatch Pitch is the competition for you that chooses as many as 12 finalists to present their business plan. All business plans are then vetted by a panel of corporate pros, such as VCs and angel investors. The competition is for SXSW in Austin. To qualify for the competition, startups should have only one product or service to launch at no later at June 30, 2014.

Prize: N/A

7. North of Boston Business Prize Competition

For companies that wish to get started in Essex County, this 21st century-powered competition makes short work of paperwork. All it needs to judge the viability of a sound business idea is to determine the quality of the plan and the people behind its execution. This competition favors participants who have great communication skills and excel at personal presentation.

Prize: 1st Place - $5,000, 2nd Place - $3,000, and 3rd Place - $2,000

8. Fast Pitch

This competition is open to students, faculty, and even local entrepreneurs. You need to make a three-minute pitch, that's all. And you will be judged on it by a panel of local leaders, academics, and investors. This competition aims to provide you coaching and feedback by experienced people to refine your idea and make it better.

Prize: $1,000 to $3,000

9. Tufts $100k Social and Classic New Venture

Available only for Tufts students, this competition aims to provide support for ideas that are at the earliest incubation stage. If you want to test the waters before committing financial and human resources to work toward an idea, this is the best program to do so.

Prize: $100k

Last, But Not the Least, Venture Funding

We could write a whole book on venture funding. For now, all you need to know is that venture capital is not easy to get and is not always a good idea. It can provide a large cash infusion if you've got a winner of a business on your hands. It does, however, require you to give up what could be a significant portion of your business.

Working With the Money You Have

Once you've got money, you need to run your business, you need to understand what to do with it. Managing money is a mystery to many people. According to a recent Bankrate.com survey, just 37% of Americans have enough savings to pay for a $500 or $1,000 emergency.

The other 63% do not have anything in savings, and would have to resort to other measures such as cutting back on spending and using a credit card in order to handle an emergency.

In business, money management is not that much better. Entrepreneurs who manage their own finances often make the same mistakes with their business finances as they do with their personal finances. Sometimes, the mistakes are even worse.

Develop a Clear Financial Plan

Many up and coming entrepreneurs get too carried away with day to day business so that they forget to take a step back and assess their business's overall financial health. Developing a clear, detailed financial plan from the beginning is an absolute must.

A solid financial plan is the foundation of every successful business as it helps entrepreneurs keep track of finances and aids in managing investments and expenses. A good financial ecosystem from the get-go may not guarantee growth and expansion, but it is certainly a necessity.

Know Your Expenses

Not even a good, well thought-out financial plan can cover all expenses. Seasoned entrepreneurs refer to these expenses as "miscellaneous expenses" - expenses that you never imagined, and that were never a part of your initial financial plan. These expenses are unexpected, a lot bigger than you imagine them to be and will definitely come.

Most entrepreneurs make the mistake of underestimating these unconventional expenses, even though they can certainly produce a powerful financial blow and jeopardize your business. Always count on miscellaneous expenses, and include them in your financial plan.

Your part-time business should also run lean. There should not be any money wasted on unnecessary items. Focus on what matters the most - substance and not style. If things go well, there is always time to buy that wonderful office furniture package you have your eye on, until then, it's better to concentrate on investing intelligently and making money. In the end, your clients and customers care a lot more about the services or product you're offering than about anything else.

Think Before Investing

Everyone expects business owners to test and think before making an investment, yet reckless, not based on empirical proof investments are a very prevalent entrepreneurial money mistake. No matter how much you like a certain product and stand behind it, there might not be a market for it.

It is always wise to analyze, think, and test the market to get some feedback before investing your time and money into something that may not even pay off in the long run. Having courage and taking risks is admirable, but being careful and taking calculated risks is what makes money.

Split personal and business finances

New entrepreneurs often fail to see the importance of having their business and personal finances separated. Perhaps they think and act like it is all their own money, which it sometimes is, but not separating finances can cause a lot of financial confusion and, in the end, create a monetary mess that can be incredibly hard to break out of. Set up different bank accounts, hire professionals to help you through the process of setting up and separating your finances, if you don't feel like you would do a good job.

Keep Backup Cash

There are many that have the philosophy that all cash in the business should be reinvested. I have even heard that entrepreneurs should not put money into retirement accounts (we'll discuss that in a second). But the very idea boggles my mind for multiple reasons.

First, it is a short sighted view that just because the sun is shining now, it will always shine. When there is a crisis, it is much better to utilize your own cash rather than borrowing. When a business has emergency cash in reserves, it is better equipped to survive an economic downturn. Borrowing when you are in trouble is a bad idea. Instead, leverage credit to grow the business. As entrepreneurs, we are good at getting ourselves out of holes.

But sometimes, it is just easier to sidestep the hole.

Another reason it is a important for your business to have backup cash is for fast expansion. Getting funding for expansion can sometimes take longer than we'd like. Whether it is from Angels or VC's, it is usually not a speedy process. Slowly building cash reserves gives you the freedom to manage your debt the right way by borrowing only what you need and then using your own cash for expansion.

Where New and Part-time Entrepreneurs Should Put Their Money

Education and Literature

As a part-time entrepreneur, this is not the area you want to get stingy. Your part-time business is your internship if you plan on leaving your job to be a full-time entrepreneur. This is your time to really learn everything you can about what could be your future.

This isn't to say you should go out and buy volumes and volumes on the history of your chosen market. Instead, look for the top selling guides to your industry. These guides can come in the form of books, monthly pamphlets, or trade magazines. Purchasing these books or subscriptions establishes you as an in the loop entrepreneur, and keeps you updated on the topical day to day happenings within your industry.

A good idea can wither if not backed with the knowledge to keep above the competition. The market research available in these kinds of literature will tell you month by month what's selling, what isn't, and what's coming next. As an added bonus, trade magazines and guide books can familiarize you with names and companies you should take note of, and prove to be a valuable tool when deciding your next networking move.

Being well read on subjects that matter to your colleagues and customers will make you an overall more knowledgeable, approachable, and respected entrepreneur. You may have faith in your vision, and the determination to become a success, but customers flock to businesses that seem to know their subject matter inside and out, making this sort of literature a must have for the competent business owner.

Memberships

Networking is crucial if you want to create a lasting company in today's media-driven world. It can be difficult to find out exactly what events to go to, and what connections to make. Look into what clubs and organizations top professionals in your industry belong to.

Something as simple as playing golf at the same club can lead to lasting bonds. People tend to trust familiar faces, and making yourself just that can be invaluable in growing your business.

Much like wearing the right clothes to cultivate your image, purchasing a membership to these professional hot spots is a personal branding move that will put your name on the map.

Search for the organizations that matter not only to the top professionals in your industry, but to people starting out at the same level as you too. Becoming well known and familiar on every level can only help you, and open doors for your company that you never dreamed possible.

The Right Tech

The "right tech" for you depends on the business you have. For some, it's quality cameras, computers, or printers. For others, it's simply purchasing the latest version of Microsoft Office. Whatever your business is, make sure that you buy and upgrade the technology needed often. This goes hand in hand with staying in the loop.

Clients looking for top quality professionals will flock to companies that use the best of the best. Ensuring that the technological side of your business is up to par will set clients' minds at ease, and keep you up to date with the latest tools available to help you succeed. Keeping up with technology of your industry is another important reason to read the literature of your field.

Trade magazines are a fantastic place to read about the technological advances that top industry professionals are utilizing, and will help you decide if those advances are right for your company.

Someone Else's Expertise

One of the things that part-time entrepreneurs need to get accustomed to is spending money for someone else's expertise. While you are learning what is vital for your business to grow, there is someone else who already knows how to do it. Just like you are paid for your expertise at your day job, it is someone else's job to do the things your business may need.

You can find people who are more skilled than you in many areas of your business. Fiverr, Upwork, and People Per hour are just a few places to look. In the beginning of your business venture, you need to focus on what you do best and outsource the rest.

Chapter 10

Getting the Word Out

"The aim of marketing is to know and understand the customer so well the product or service fits him and sells itself."

-Peter Drucker

By now, you've probably concluded that as a part-time entrepreneur, there are certain things that you must do to succeed. Part-time entrepreneurship is very different than full-time entrepreneurship in many ways. But when it comes to some of the essential elements that create a successful business, the difference between the two types of entrepreneurship disappears.

One of those essential elements is how an entrepreneur of any kind lets the others know about the product or service that is for sale. The way you choose to market your business will be a major determining factor in the success of your venture. In this chapter, we will look at different ways part-time entrepreneurs can market their business.

Yes, You Do Need a Marketing Plan

Marketing is a buzz word that is a central focus of startups as well as established businesses. You, as a part-time entrepreneur, should make it a point of focus as well. A marketing plan is a blueprint that maps out the advertising efforts that a company will perform during the year.

This plan indicates the business processes that are going to be performed so as to achieve set marketing targets within a specific time period. A marketing plan can be short, brief, and straight to the point. On the other hand, it can be long and require hundreds of pages when printed. Some marketing plans are very affordable to produce, while others are a bit pricey.

The scope of your marketing plan determines how big and exhaustive it will be.

One of the main characteristics of this plan is that it is fluid. This means that it can be adjusted so as to accommodate emerging changes in the market or the business environment.

The marketing plan should be created after conducting research, and identifying the attainable results, as well as performing strategic positioning.

The marketing plan guides the activities of the department and all involved stakeholders for a number of months or years. As such, the parties involved should understand that this plan can be changed so as to accommodate the business environment. Every marketing plan should have some specific parts in it.

Your plan should include these things:

The Point of it ALL

Every business effort has some goals. They should always be quantifiable. This means that you should be able to convert these goals into numbers. An example of a goal is that you want to sell 100 products in the first week of release. These goals can be described as sales, profit margin, or satisfaction of your customers.

Well Defined Marketing Budget

Marketing can get expensive if you do not budget correctly. From print ads, online, and PR, a small marketing budget can balloon due to the numerous ways to market your business. You should indicate the cost of marketing your product or service. Also, indicate if you will perform in-house marketing or you will outsource it.

Market Research Data

This part has information about the target market of the product or the service. This information should contain details such as the dynamics of the target market, their purchasing patterns, any seasonality involved, as well as any demographic data. In addition to that, this segment of the marketing plan should have an outline indicating the segment of the market that you want to target, their needs, and their purchasing decision-making process, as well as the competitor products already in the market.

The market research segment of this plan should have the current sales of the competition, their prices as well as any and all benchmarks that are involved. It should also contain the suppliers that you intend to work with. The data that is included in this segment should be detailed, exhaustive, and current. This is because it will guide the efforts of the marketing department.

According to Victoria Treyger, CMO of Kabbage, conducting extensive market research is not only inexpensive, but also crucial for your businesses marketing strategy. Research your target market, the characteristics of your target market, so that you can know what kind of messages and advertisement media is most appropriate for them. You should also research your competitors' marketing strategy and their weaknesses. This will help you determine the best way of growing your business.

A Description of the Target Market

Find niche or target markets for your product and describe them. The niche market that you are targeting should also be described in the marketing plan. Research about the target market should be conducted and the data found must be included in the plan. Identify and describe the target market as well as you can. After that, include this information in the marketing plan.

Details about your Product

Give a detailed description of your product or service. Also, give information about how it can benefit the market. Does it fill a gap in the market? Does it create a new need? Are there are any other products or services currently servicing the same need? These questions should be answered in this part of the marketing plan. In addition to that, you can look to see if your product offers something special over and above similar ones in the market.

Information About Your Competition

Every sector of business that has more than one player has some competition in it. There are always high chances that the sector that you are entering has competition for your product. Thus, your marketing plan should include details such as the unique selling position that you want to take. In this plan, indicate the factors of your product that will make you stand out uniquely among your competition. In addition to that, observe and see how your competition has conducted branding. Are you doing the same or taking a different, more successful direction? This information should be in this section of the plan.

The Marketing Strategy that you are Employing

Every marketing effort follows a specific marketing strategy. This is a plan of execution. In this section of the plan, you should indicate the marketing strategy that you want to use for your product or service. This section should also indicate the promotion methods that you intend to use.

There are many unique marketing strategies that you can utilize today.

Examples of these are:

- Online Presence; today, this is a strategy that you must apply. In this digital age, consumers are heading to the Internet to search for products or services. Create a website for your item or service. In addition to that, it will be very beneficial if you market and promote the website online too.

- Forming networks; this is where you physically go to the areas where your market is located, meet them, and form profitable relationships.

- Marketing directly; this is where you use media such as flyers, brochures, and sales letters to convey information about your product.

- Content Marketing; in this strategy, you can begin by writing information about your product or service, and the market environment of your product, as well as any new information about it. This will get you identified as an expert on the product or service. This reputation drives sales when your product hits the shelves. This strategy should be conducted long before you hit the market with your product.

- Personal selling; in this strategy, you go directly to your market and sell them the product or service first hand.

- General advertising; in this strategy, you conduct marketing in print media and other directories to inform your target market of the product.

Marketing and Advertising for the Part-Time Entrepreneur

When it comes to building a successful business, advertising is among the most valuable tools available to entrepreneurs. Large companies shell out millions of dollars a year to keep their ventures in the public eye, and information readily available to the masses.

For part-time entrepreneurs without large advertising budgets, this practice can be a daunting source of frustration and can leave business owners feeling that their company is not getting the spotlight it deserves. This is especially tough for new businesses. Fortunately, there are resources for free publicity available to business owners that are willing to broaden their horizons and think outside of the box.

Social Media Groups and Pages

Social media outlets offer business owners an opportunity to reach thousands of potential customers for little to no money. Creating a Facebook, Instagram, or Twitter account for your business can draw in customers on a local or global scale. It gives you, as a business owner, the chance to share events, press releases, sales, and other information about your company while also allowing customers to express opinions and ask questions.

These kinds of accounts allow for a more personal connection between companies and the people that utilize their services. Social media also gives entrepreneurs a chance to see what fans are looking for, collect data, and check out the competition. Beyond typical accounts, try implementing a company blog, and posting content to YouTube.

The more your company is seen and heard of, the more traffic your accounts will get. According to a recent survey, nearly two-thirds of Americans use social media on a daily basis. Bringing your company to the social media age will allow you to advertise to these two-thirds, and draw in significant new revenue.

Social media can be leveraged to help you market your business for a small fee or even at no cost at all. For example, you can invest about $41-$71 on sponsored links on either Facebook or LinkedIn. Such an investment will help place your brand across hundreds of thousands of your target audience. The goal is to increase followers to your social media accounts, or to convert visits into sales.

It is possible to gain a lot of attention if your social media profile produces something that goes viral. However, to better your odds of getting followers and fans, use the available advertising options.

Local Libraries

Perhaps it has been a while since you've visited your local library. Even so, libraries remain a hub for senior citizens and families with young children. For these demographics, among others, libraries are a hub of the community and a place to go to gather new information. This makes them an important base to cover when it comes to utilizing all of the resources available to your company. **Many libraries are willing to post fliers and informational pamphlets to help local businesses thrive for free**.

They make this information public via their bulletin boards and front desks. Libraries are also a center for people looking for employment. If your company is one that offers services in that vein, or that caters to these demographics, they are absolutely a can't miss opportunity.

College Campus Fairs and Newspapers

Every college campus offers several special interest fairs a year. They are similar to libraries in the case of free advertising. Businesses such as personal training, health, home décor, computer or job training, and cleaning services can be very useful to college students, and the professors and visitors that spend their time on campus.

College fairs (especially around move-in times) are a great place to advertise to students that may need your company's services at some point in the year. As an added bonus, college newspapers and radio stations are always looking for new partners. If not free, these campuses offer extremely cheap publicity to large numbers of young people each year.

Referrals and Word of Mouth

Referrals are the age-old advertising trick that has kept businesses going from long before the information age. Having vocal fans of your business is a surefire way to draw in new customers that already feel a sense of connection to your company.

Offer discounts and benefits to customers who refer friends, and cultivate a business that helps spread itself. Be sure that your customers understand the integrity and mission of your company, so that if asked about it, they feel excited to share a great idea with friends and family. But you don't just wait around for referrals, ask for them!

Internet and Local Directories

There are lots of directories such as Google, Yahoo, Yellow Pages, and Craigslist that allow businesses to share information with potential clients by giving them a direct contact line. It is critical that potential clients know how to contact your business, operating hours, and location.

Having this information readily available and easy to access is a key step to creating a pleasant experience between your clientele and your company. Many of these directories offer free or incredibly cheap deals to post your information on a global scale.

Be sure to utilize these sites, and keep the contact information you post updated and consistent. These sites are also hubs for gathering ratings. A good rating is the best free advertising a company can get, and helps clients find your company.

No matter what your business specializes in, advertising everywhere and often can only be beneficial. Keep your eyes open for opportunities both online and within your own community to create more buzz and expand your business's clientele horizons.

"Celebrity" Endorsements

The term "celebrity" has changed in the past 10 years or so. Celebrity used to mean someone on TV or movies who are followed around by paparazzi and pose for the red carpet. Celebrity these days can be a 15 year old who posts videos on YouTube. In fact, the power of famous bloggers and on YouTubers has changed the way companies seek endorsements.

One of the easiest ways to get your brand noticed is to get celebrities to endorse your product. This is one of the best ways to market your business for free, especially if your business entails making wearable products. Send free samples of your products to celebrities who you think will appreciate your brand and reflect it well. Celebrities have the potential to drive more sales by getting their fans to buy a certain product that they like.

As a small company, you can give your product to bloggers and vloggers for them to try. If they like your product, they will usually review the product and present it to their followers.

Write for Local Publications

One of the best ways to get free advertisement is to get local publications to feature your story. Write to local publications requesting them to feature your new business since you are a local person. Local publications like local stories, and they are bound to feature your business if you prove to have an interesting story. Alyssa Smith founded luxury jewelry brand Alyssa Smith Jewelry in 2009, and was eventually named "Entrepreneur of the Year." When starting her business, she used many low cost ways to market her company.

Alyssa Smith wrote to magazines and asked if she could write a column on "how I started my business or the tribulations of being a small business owner." This slowly started getting her company some recognition. Later, bigger magazines were able to feature her business and by so doing, won her business even more free advertising.

Chapter 11

Learning to Sell

"In sales, it's not what you say; it's how they perceive what you say."

-Jeffrey Gitomer

Depending on your business, where you sell is going to vary. You may have a product that will be exclusively on Amazon, your e-commernce store, Esty, or Facebook. Keep in mind that these outlets help you make the sale, they do not sell for you. Because of this fact, you will need to learn how to sell to your customers. Let's start with how to sell to people directly.

Pitching to People

Let's start with selling to individuals. Remember that your co-workers, family, and friends may turn out to be your first and best customers. There is also the possibility that you will run into people who you are not very close with who may still want to buy from you.

At some point in time, or at a lot of points, we've all been asked the question, "So what is it that you do?" As entrepreneurs, this question carries the subtext of, "So what is that your startup actually does?"

Whether it's an extended family member at the holidays, a friend you haven't caught up with in a while, or even a potential investor, you only have a short amount of time to give them an answer that gives a broad enough view of your business but is specific enough to be engaging. The way that you answer this question may be the make or break point in selling your idea to others.

The sixty-second elevator pitch has been heralded as the key to providing these answers, but entrepreneurs need to move beyond this type of pitch to accurately convey their identity in long-form answers. Your elevator pitch can get your foot in the door with a potential investor, but won't cut it in any investor meeting. Likewise, a sixty-second pitch isn't enough to accurately convey your business model, culture, and presence to the media or to your customers.

Start With the Problem

A good business pitch identifies the problem that your startup solves for potential consumers and offers a real solution to that problem. Too many of us start with a solution: the product or service that we know we want to offer and work backwards towards a problem. But if this solution doesn't actually solve a problem that people have, it's rendered useless. Your solution has to address a problem head-on, but this problem also has to resonate with a sizeable target market.

Simply, your solution needs to address a problem that a significant amount of people have. The problem that your solution tackles should be one that other people have. Here it can be helpful to run focus groups and market research to see whether others agree that it is a problem. Identifying, and then conveying those findings to others, your target market requires balance.

While the temptation may be to identify large potential markets that encompass significant proportions of a population, you run the risk of losing credibility. If your solution can only reach a small niche group, such as adults living in the Pacific Northwest who have dogs or some other extremely specific group, investors will be hesitant to supply you with the capital you need when they see little room to grow their ROI.

Tailoring Your Pitch

At this point, your pitch will need to be tailored to your audience. A writer who is covering your launch needs less information about your inner financial workings than an investor will. Likewise, your friends at a social gathering don't need to know your strategy for building a team to carry out your vision.

Investors want to know how much capital you need, how you will use it, and when they can expect to see milestones being reached. Here, your business model needs to reflect your profit/loss margins, costs, cash flow, and your current balance sheet. Your sales projection, or your forecast for future sales, doesn't necessarily need to be a detailed five-year plan. It should, however, be limited to a certain time frame.

They will also want to know how you plan to address your competition. Every startup has competition. Even if you truly think that you've found a solution that addresses a problem that no other business is currently addressing, consumers are creating their own workarounds.

The one exception may be related to solutions that address new technology, but the competition for these solutions is fierce. What makes you the right startup to address these problems? In what ways will you offer a better solution than the ones that are already on the market?

A successful pitch takes careful planning, due diligence, thoughtfulness, and practice. We can see how our product will improve the lives of our customers, but if we aren't able to present our solution in a compelling pitch it does us no good. As Peter Coughter wrote in The Art of the Pitch, "We all fall in love with our own ideas. The trick is to know when to fall out of love with these ideas and get out of the presentation."

Selling Online

AMAZON AND EBAY SELLING

If you are just starting out on the road to making a great living from selling goods online, one of the first questions you might ask yourself is simply eBay and Amazon - what's the difference? These two websites dominate the buying and selling marketplace when it comes to the Internet, but they both operate in very different ways.

1. Auctions vs. Fixed Price Goods

Perhaps the most obvious difference between these two giant websites is how items are actually sold. Head over to eBay and you'll notice plenty of Auction style listings, where you place a bid for the amount you are willing to pay for the item in question. Even Buy It Now listings on eBay, which provide more of a fixed alternative to this auction style, often come complete with an option for a buyer to put in their best offer.

Amazon, on the other hand, offers buyers a fixed rate. There's no arguing, no waiting for auctions to finish, and no doubt as to how much money you will make for a product that sells on this website.

2. Individuals vs. an Organization

Many who don't know much about the logistics of buying and selling on the Internet assume that eBay is made up solely of individuals, trying to sell off some goods that may or may not have fallen off the back of a truck! Of course, we know that this isn't the case and that there are many fully fledged businesses just using eBay as their shop front. Unfortunately though, this is the reputation that eBay continues to fight against.

A lot of people frequently misunderstand the operation of Amazon in a similar, though entirely more beneficial, way. As Amazon is a large organization that holds vast amounts of stock itself, a lot of buyers simply don't realize that the purchase they just made actually did come from an individual rather than Amazon itself. Every time you list an item for sale on Amazon, you are benefiting from the positive reputation that this sales giant brings to the table. Your buyers know that they can expect great customer service and a clear pricing strategy simply because your products are flown beneath the "Amazon" banner.

3. The Customer Base

There are a multitude of differences between these two websites, but one of the most obvious is that of the customer base.

Customers visiting the Amazon website tend to be very loyal for several reasons:

- They know that the Amazon website, or an Amazon marketplace vendor, is almost certain to offer what they want. With such a diverse range of categories and goods it is possible to get your hands on almost anything you want without ever leaving Amazon.

- Amazon runs an incredibly clever direct marketing campaign, sending emails to former buyers containing links to products that they might want in the future. That's not to say that visitors to the eBay website can't be just as loyal, but it is always worth bearing in mind that every time you list a new product for sale on the Amazon website, there will be a group of loyal customers that will never even consider looking elsewhere.

Both Amazon and eBay have their own benefits. Some products sell better on one website, some better on another, so if you really want to maximize your earning potential online, you should consider operating out of both.

Beginners Guide to Starting a Profitable Business on eBay and Amazon

When it comes to online commerce, nothing beats eBay and Amazon. These two are the most popular online sales companies on the Internet, with revenues going through the roof. In 2015, eBay generated $8.46 billion in revenues, while Amazon posted an all-time high profit of $19.166.

Selling on eBay and Amazon is definitely one of the most profitable ways to make money. Your goal is to become a prominent merchant selling top quality products and not just a casual auction guy selling items from your garage. This isn't an easy task. At some point, you're going to run into stumbling blocks, such as competition, lack of market demand, not enough customers, etc. But if you know how to navigate your way through these challenges, selling on eBay and Amazon will prove to be a profitable business.

How to find promising merchandise that guarantees only success? Many entrepreneurs out there end up losing a great deal of their investment because of their lame approach to doing business. If there is but one rule about online selling it is "keeping up with the times."

Here you will learn surefire techniques on profitable online marketing and how to be a sales magnet on eBay and Amazon.

The keys to online selling

As with any business, the key to a successful eBay career is understanding the market. Don't sell products that don't sell. Conduct thorough research on the items that are popular with the masses. Suppose you plan to sell flip-flops, ask yourself, do I actually have a market for this? What makes my brand a cut above the rest? If you get to a point where you can honestly say that you have a market, then you can move on to the next step.

The next step is to know your competition well enough. How much do they sell the same item for? What is the going rate for such items? Don't list your product at an opening price which is totally way out of line. Let customers get a feel of the product, by writing compelling descriptions about it. If buyers are critical enough when buying in an actual store, just imagine how overtly critical they can get when purchasing online. Provide a close-up picture of the product and explain in detail its size, color, weight, and texture.

Online sellers are treated as scammers by default. They are known to be naturally deceptive, and so people don't just trust them right off the bat. Respect is something that you have to earn when selling on the virtual world of the Internet. To earn trust and respect, be overly professional in everything. Conduct proper business from the get-go. This means following protocols, proper business ethics, charging proper taxes, and carefully tweaking minute details such as the make and packaging of the product. If you get good reviews, the good news spreads fast like a disease. Positive feedback is a priceless thing when promoting online merchandise.

Tips To Help You Make Money from EBay and Amazon

There's always a learning curve to any business, and eBay and Amazon, are no exception. Like most new business owners, you will face teething problems. You may be worried about situations you thought were unique to you, and spent long hours looking for answers to problems you thought would jeopardize your business now and in the future. It happens to everyone and not long afterwards, we all look back on those days and wonder why we worried so much, and why we wasted time looking for answers to problems that really weren't that important.

Things to Sell On EBay to Make Money - 3 Steps to Find "Killer" Products Now

What things to sell on eBay to make money... there might not be a more asked "how to get rich from the Internet" question today.

This might be the best online business to start today.

There are two ways you can earn on the site... selling physical and digital products. There are a lot of courses on how to sell digital products on eBay... and this used to be a very valid method.

But since they switched to the "classified ads" format, its become much more difficult to sell digital products. I supposed you can still make it work, but I wouldn't recommend it-it's much easier to sell physical products.

So how do you find the "right" physical products to sell and get rich off the Internet? Here are three steps to locate them now.

Focus on "SPECIFIC NICHES"

What's a "specific niche"? Juicers, blenders, dehydrators, etc. the market as a whole would be "health," but you would never sell something to the whole health community because it's simply too broad.

The key is to be as focused as possible... this is how to find things to sell on eBay to make money. Use those "specific" keywords in your auctions as well.

Sure, you might get more traffic by targeting the term "weight loss"--but it's going to be less targeted and therefore probably won't sell as well.

Get wholesale catalogs BEFORE researching

This is critical because

*It gives you more ideas for what to sell..."

*it also assures that you will be able to sell the product." Most people just research any and every product they can think of BEFORE finding a wholesaler... which means that they often waste hours of effort on a product they can't sell anyway.

Do THOROUGH product research

Failure to do this has been the downfall of many online auction business plans. When researching the product, make sure it sells for an average price that will be profitable for you and that a high enough percentage of the auctions succeed.

Remember, the average selling price for a product might be $25... but if only 33% of the auctions sell, then you can only plan on making about $8/auction. This is how to find the best things to sell on eBay to make money.

The Business of Amazon Book Reseller

Amazon.com is a website which millions of individuals venture to each day to make purchases. Many of the industry's leading retailers have their websites linked to Amazon as it draws so many viewers. One of the nice features here is that individuals can resell their products. What is also nice is that Amazon features these on the searches that people do for related products. This means that individuals can choose to pay full price or they can go with a used product.

For those who have bookcases of books (you know you are out there) that you have read, or planned to read about ten years ago, there may be a market for them. If you have dusty books that are in decent shape (always make sure they are not musty or mildewed) you may find that Amazon is the ideal location for you to find a way to get rid of them and earn some money for it.

The process is quite simple. You will first need to list with Amazon as a seller. This is a free and easy step that will take only a few minutes. Next, sit down with a stack of books that you would like to sell. All you need to do is list the title and author on the website and Amazon does all the rest for you. They provide all the details of the book to the viewers. Like eBay, Amazon will charge you a percentage of the amount that you sell the book for. But, unlike eBay, this is not an auction but just a listing service. You are not charged anything until the book (or other item) sells.

In order to make it profitable, it is necessary for the individual to research how well the books of this type or by this author are selling. You do not want to go so high as to keep the book from being sold but you don't want to go so low as to undermine your profitability. This research is simple to do on Amazon as well.

Don't have any books to sell? You simply need to check out the wide range of options open to you in your local area. For example, there are often garage sales filled with books (again, make sure they aren't smelly!) Or, you can visit a thrift shop or other secondhand type stores, giveaways, or even the bargain bin at your local bookstore. Even secondhand bookstores are a great way to buy cheap books which you can resell at a profit!

Another way that you can earn an income from Amazon if you are a webmaster includes earning an income for referral fees. If you refer others to come to Amazon, you can earn a little extra income too. You can learn more about how to do this right on the website.

The process is simple, and the rewards are fairly good. There are no outright costs to becoming an Amazon book reseller and much to be gained. In fact, it is a decent way to easily make a second income from home. Gather up those dusty books and begin your search for money through Amazon.com reseller programs.

Pricing Your Product and Services

Pricing is one of the things that determine the success of your business. If you want to be clear about what you want to achieve, then it is high time you came up with a good pricing strategy. The main reason why you are doing business is to make money. Therefore, you cannot afford to choose a wrong pricing strategy. The worst mistake that you can make is to believe that the price you are going to choose will drive your sales. Instead, the ability of selling your products is what will drive your sales. Therefore, it is wise to hire the right persons to help you when it comes to marketing as well as adopt the best pricing strategies.

Underpricing

Underpricing greatly affected the profit made by the manufacturer. Although there are very many investors who believe that this is the best step when the economy is down, this is not always the case. When pricing your products you need to know that accuracy is very important in any economic cycle. Many investors tend to underprice their products in an attempt to convince buyers that they are selling inexpensive products. Remember that every consumer wants to believe that he or she is getting the worth of his or her money, hence you need to take care of all the costs when it comes to pricing products.

Overpricing

A good example of overpriced products is the 1963 Pontiac Catalina – $ 48,000. Many people thought that the high price of this vehicle was a result of clerical error, but it was never the case. Although it is a rare muscle car, the price is too high. Overpricing of this product had detrimental effects on buyers, especially those who look at the products from competitors. When you price your products beyond the desire of your consumers, it will reduce your sales. Consumers will think that you want to cover the expenses of your employees by overpricing.

Simple steps on how to price your products

There are different ways that you can use when it comes to pricing your products. To be very successful, you should combine different tools and understand that the main factor you need to take into account is your customer. The more you understand your customer's needs, the better you will be positioned to offer them the value of their money. Here are tips on how to price your products.

Step 1-Understand your customer's needs

You need to undertake market research before deciding on the price of your products. This research can include sending an email and conducting informal surveys. If you do not have money to spend on market research, simply look at various groups. You need to figure out the segment you are targeting as well as pricing before making your final decision.

Step 2-Understand your costs

One of the fundamental tenets when it comes to product pricing is to understand your costs. You should cover all the expenses, and then factor in the amount of profit you are likely to get at the end of the day. In addition, you should know how much you need to mark up your products and the price you should sell them in order to make more profits.

The cost of the product is often higher than the literal cost of the item because it includes the overhead costs of the same product. The overhead costs of your products can include fixed and variable costs such as shipping as well as stocking fees, among others. It is good to include all these cost when coming up with prices for your products. Failing to take into account all these factors is likely to lead to underpricing of your products, something that will affect your sales.

Step 3- Revenue Target

How much revenue do you want? You need to know your revenue target when producing, marketing, and selling different products. Targeting your revenue can be very complex, especially when you are dealing in a wide range of products. Start by estimating the number of units you wish to sell before the end of the day.

Divide your target revenue with the sum of units you are expecting to sell, and you know the price that you should sell in order to attain your profit goals. In case you are dealing in different products, you should allocate the overall revenue you are targeting by each of the products.

Step 4-Competition

It is very helpful to a look at your competitors when pricing your products. You customers will compare your price to that of your competitors before making their purchases. Find out whether the products are sold at prices comparable to yours. You can only set higher prices if your products are highly priced when compared to those sold by your competitors. Be very cautious about the differences brought about the region. It can be worthwhile to undertake a head to head comparison of different products with those of your competitors. While doing so, ensure that you use the net prices for accurate results.

Step 5- Direction of the market

Keeping track of the market direction will help you to determine the demand of your products. You should look at the long term weather patterns and laws of the country among other factors before fixing the price of your products. In addition, you need to understand that your competitors are likely to respond to your prices by introducing new products in the market.

Raising and lowering of product prices

• When to raise Prices- It is wise to test new prices, offers as well as combinations that can help to sell more products at better prices. You can raise your prices and then offer special customer services or unique bonuses to boost your sales. Ensure that you measure the decrease or increase in the amount of products you are going to sell as well as the gross profit. The best way to find out whether you have priced your products correctly is looking at the sales volume.

• When to Lower Prices -You are likely to miss your target audience by overpricing your products. You can decide to include discounts or give your customers free products to increase the volume of your sales.

It's hard being a startup. You've just embarked on a crazy as rails business idea which may or may not succeed, depending on a variety of factors. Do the people like your new product? Are they ready for this new and jazzy service which can potentially revolutionize lives in an instant? Questions such as these keep entrepreneurs awake at night and burning the midnight oil and for good reason too. This is because the success of these ideas and their execution can mean all the difference between make and break.

One thing is for sure. Startups need to do great on lead generation and sales. There's no two ways about it. And it's an issue that many founders of a new product or service don't devote energies on, seeing as how their own enthusiasm for their baby lets them get carried away to issues such as customer needs and requirements.

But all is not lost. There are ways to sell your product, solution, or service to the market in a way that just gets the customers. Startups can make their products or services marketable that truly speak to consumers, the natural, effortless, and authentic way. The case of misplaced idealism founders are usually associated with can be sidestepped. Just because they have a zealous faith in their idea doesn't necessarily make them a sales guru (exceptions such as Steve Jobs exist, but even he faced the same issue with the Apple Lisa).

That being said, every startup entrepreneur can get superior lead generation and sales if they keep in mind the following things:

Find the Right Audience (And Companies) That Seem Interested In What You Have To Offer

Startups, in a bid to get far ahead of themselves, tend to overdo a simple thing; they sell their solutions to everyone, irrespective of whether they are the perfect fit for your product/services or not. **Not only is this a waste of time and money, it's a waste of efforts which could've been focused on cultivating the right customers and companies**. It is important for startups to do their market research, and see which companies align perfectly with your messaging, marketing, product, and services.

It is also important to make your product/service fit for a limited trial run. Giving people a chance to try out the next big thing your startup came up with is a surefire way to build up authenticity and credibility in this cutthroat business climate. Time matters. Plus, your leads come in easily as they have something to try out and talk about.

Categorize Your Leads

So, you've got a sizeable number of leads? Good. Because now there's a need to have a solid mechanism in place – a system to track and rank those leads in terms of popularity and interest. Every company worth its name does this. And it accomplishes it by using a Customer Relation Management System (CRM) which tracks and updates leads and updates information about them over time. It's a system which can serve as a centralized resource for collecting all information and data pertaining to a prospect – conversations, evaluations, taking-action, follow-ups, and more. It's an efficient means to track the sales process.

The issue with CRMs is they are expensive, something a startup can't afford in the initial stages. But hope isn't lost, as lead tracking and monitoring can be done without investing a pretty penny. A spreadsheet to keep track of leads and classifying them easily into high priority to normal priority items is a good idea.

You can also use the spreadsheet to detail every contact and conversation you've had with them, thus beginning a process of nurturing the prospect over a period of time.

The important thing to note is that even though you might not be immediately getting a sale from the prospect, building a long-term relationship with a lead can result in more leads coming your way. It's important to follow-up with the prospective buyers at regular intervals in time. Keeping a note of their queries, their answers, and other assorted information is a good way to figure out what people demand of your product or service.

People Hate Sales Pitch: Period!

Ask any man or woman on the street, and salespersons get all the hate in the world for good reason. Salespeople are more concerned with selling the products or services irrespective of whether people really need them. Hence the bad rep that is directed their way. This is something most startups and their founders think is abhorrent.

So, if a sales pitch is out of the picture, how can you convince the customer to buy the new product or service you're offering?

Here's how:

Identify the needs of the customer.

Build relationships with the customer which extend beyond the "buy it and forget it" mentality.

Align your startup's goals and wares with those of the customer and their needs (Be customer-centric).

Demonstrate value which comes when people choose your product over the competitors.

Have a conversation, not a droning on and on sales pitch.

Connect With Customers

It used to be that companies made a product and people had little choice but to buy it because there were no alternatives out there. But now, in the age of social media and mobile communications, consumer perception has undergone a massive change, making the businesses of yesteryears to be receptive of what people demand from them.

Simply put, this is the age where companies can reap more rewards if they take a collaborative approach to sales – listening to customers, incorporating their suggestions and feedback into your products and services. Iterating and perfecting your product all the way so people get their money's worth, and then some more.

Startups need to rely more on what consumers want. Connecting with them straightaway guarantees a ready market for your products/services/solutions. And besides, startups are not in it solely for the money. They have their credibility, their reputation, and their business to protect. This is how companies can ensure their future success when their product takes off. Consumer goodwill is now playing a huge part in making or breaking startups, thanks to social media technologies and trends.

For every startup that succeeds, there are 50 more that have not taken off. In this climate, it is important to have a good business plan for your startup so the probability of going the way of the dodo is minimized.

Conclusion

We hope you enjoy and have found value in these pages. For more insight on entrepreneurship, startups, technology, productivity and more, please visit http://startupmindset.com

Made in the USA
San Bernardino, CA
09 April 2020